VICTORIAN PATCHWORK

VICTORIAN PATCHWORK

FREDA PARKER

Photography by Di Lewis

BROCKHAMPTON PRESS
LONDON

First published in Great Britain in 1991
by Anaya Publishers Ltd, Strode House
44–50 Osnaburgh Street
London NW1 3ND

This edition published 1995 by Brockhampton Press,
a member of Hodder Headline PLC Group.

Frontispiece: 'Going to Bed' by John Burgess
(1814–74). Bridgeman Art Library
Endpapers: Detail of quilt shown on page 101, from
the Beamish Open Air Museum, Co. Durham,
photography by Di Lewis

Editor: Eve Harlow
Designer: Sheila Volpe
Picture Researcher: Andrea Stem
Artwork: Mike Leaman and Cilla Ulrick

British Library Cataloguing in Publication Data
Parker, Freda
Victorian Patchwork
1. Title
746.46

ISBN 1 86019 193 2

Typeset by Chapterhouse,
The Cloisters, Formby, Nr Liverpool L37 3PX
Colour reproduction by Columbia Offset, Singapore
Printed and bound by Oriental Press, Dubai

CONTENTS

INTRODUCTION

Patchwork is a very ancient craft with its origins going back into the mists of antiquity. Little has survived, however, from before the eighteenth century and most of the pieces still in existence are nineteenth-century work. There is still quite a wealth of articles from this era to be found in museums and collections and even tucked away in the cupboards and attics of private houses.

Then, as now, there were basically two different types of patchwork made – with or without papers (see page 96). With the first, the 'English method', small, geometric shapes which had previously been basted to thin card were oversewn together. Often a single shape, a hexagon or diamond for example, was used to cover a whole bedcover in a repeat pattern. The hexagon in particular lent itself to a variety of designs. Sometimes two or more shapes were combined to give yet more patterns. It was not usual for this type of patchwork to be quilted. Often the fabrics used were luxurious silks and velvets.

With the second type of patchwork, the 'American method', the patches were seamed together with running stitches. Shapes were usually simple squares, rectangles and triangles and might be quite large. This type of work was normally quilted. This method of piecing was, and is, the one most commonly used in the United States of America, but it was also very popular in the North of England, in Wales and in Ireland. In 1856, Singer patented the first domestic sewing machine and from this time much of this type of patchwork was made by machine.

The American method was the most usual one used for making medallion quilts in which a central design was surrounded by a series of borders. It was also used for strip patchwork, where lengthways strips made up of squares and triangles were alternated with plain strips. In addition, the technique was used for making the block patterns which were used in British patchwork but for which the United States of America is especially famed.

A third method of making patchwork is to apply the patches to a backing fabric, as with Log Cabin and Crazy Patchwork. These were both very popular in the Victorian era – the latter became very much the rage on both sides of the Atlantic from about 1860.

There was a definite toing and froing of patchwork patterns between the Old and New Worlds. Most likely, the early American settlers took the craft with them from their old home, but over the years it developed into a very distinctive national craft with a character all its own. During the second half of the nineteenth century the flow of ideas went the other way and the American influence can be seen on British work from that time. The Beamish Museum in County Durham, England has several examples. One particularly striking quilt was made by Phoebe Watson who probably never left her home in Weardale. But her sister Phyllis had emigrated to America and sent patterns home to her.

In former times, when fabric was difficult to come by, patchwork had been a way of preserving the merest scraps of precious material. In America, which in the days of the early settlers had no textile industry of its own and little access to fabrics from abroad, this was particularly the case and recycling was very much the order of the day. Even feed sacks were washed and dyed to make patches for quilts.

By the time Queen Victoria ascended the British throne in 1837, however, fabric was generally far more plentiful and mass-produced cottons were readily available. Dress prints in all-over, small, floral patterns were particularly popular. Woollen cloth was also used for making quilts, often the left-over off-cuts, or 'fents', from factories, or the best bits cut from discarded jackets and trousers. The

The Victorian parlour had a cosy feel with its glowing fire and abundance of drapery – at the windows, over the mantelpiece and on the *chaise-longue*

richly-coloured felty fabrics from old military uniforms also frequently reappeared as patchwork footstools or slippers.

Cotton was most frequently the choice for north of England quilts and pastel colours were most popular. In Wales, more robust colours were favoured – reds, dark blues and maroons – and patchwork quilts were often made from wool.

One colour combination which had very wide appeal was Turkey Red and white. The secret of making the brilliant Turkey Red dye was discovered in the late eighteenth century. Its charm lay in the fact that it was colour-fast and did not fade but kept 'bright and fresh to the last'.

Towards the end of the century it was possible to buy bags of fabric scraps especially for patchwork. Averil Colby, writing in the 1950s, quotes an old lady who, as a young child (c. 1890) was sent out to buy 'a pennyworth of patches all done up in a bag ready to be stitched together'.

Patchwork was made by people from all walks of life. In rural districts it was still very much linked with thrift and economy. Mostly, people made bedcovers, interlined and quilted for warmth.

This Turkey Red and white cotton signature coverlet was made as a fund raiser for the Methodist chapel in Lanchester, County Durham, in the north of England, to celebrate Edward VII's coronation in 1901

Quilting was a means of holding the layers together with lines of running stitches, often in beautiful and intricate patterns. Clothing and furnishings were recycled to make patchwork quilts and often old quilts were themselves reused as fillings for new ones.

Mothers often made patchwork quilts as wedding presents for their daughters and young girls would make patchwork bedcovers for their bottom drawers, or hope chests. Sometimes, the covers would not be finally made up into quilts until the girls became engaged.

Quilting was frequently a group activity. This might just involve the members of the family, all taking a hand in the work with the small children kept busy threading needles. But sometimes friends would be asked to help and the event would turn into a pleasant social occasion with a great deal of conversation and laughter. In Ireland this was known as a quilting and in America it was called a quilting bee, where it was immortalized in song by the composer Stephen Foster:

> *Twas from Aunt Dinah's quilting party*
> *I was seein' Nellie home!*

'The Wedding Quilt' by Ralph Hedley, 1883, shows a Victorian family hard at work creating a patchwork wedding quilt as a gift to be cherished

Dressmakers might take up patchwork as a sideline and women in impoverished circumstances sometimes made and sold patchwork articles. In the north of England, where some of the finest quilting was done, widows, and the wives of men injured in mining accidents, frequently kept their families by means of their needles.

Ladies with a more leisurely lifestyle took up patchwork as a branch of fancy-work. They used silks, satins and brocades to produce articles for the parlour rather than the bedroom – cushions, covers for chair seats and piano stools, antimacassars, fire screens, teapot and egg cosies, workbags and pin cushions. Some pieces were made up of hundreds of tiny hexagons, painstakingly joined by hand and, often, patchwork was embellished – even smothered – with embroidery and beads. Although such articles can hardly be described as the basic necessities of life, making them from scraps of fabric gave Victorian ladies a comfortable feeling that they, too, were being thrifty and useful.

9

Patchwork was taught in schools in Britain, Ireland and in America as part of a training for the poor in 'plain sewing'. On one Irish estate, children were taught patchwork in school and then made bedcovers which they exchanged for essentials at the estate shop.

Many men have been involved in patchwork. Husbands and fathers often helped design the pattern and would also cut out the templates for their wives and daughters for both patchwork and quilting. Some men even made patchwork quilts – Samuel Ross, whose work can be seen on pages 20–21, is just one of many. Soldiers and sailors are particularly associated with patchwork for some reason, often producing very intricate work. In some cases, it was taught to injured soldiers as a method of occupational therapy.

A soldier who took up patchwork for a rather different reason was Private Roberts. He used it as a cure for intemperance! *The British Workman* magazine, in an issue dated 1870, takes up this moral tale:

...Roberts resolved to give up the drink and abandon the canteen. His duties left him more than a usual amount of leisure. He at once said to himself, 'I must be employed, or I shall get into mischief.' He had not been much accustomed to the use of the needle, but he resolved to *try*. First he made pincushions and smaller pieces of patchwork. Then he resolved to make a quilt. Not finding all the colours required, he solved the difficulty by dyeing the pieces the colour he needed... The second quilt he made at Aldershot [a military town in the south of England]. Shortly after its completion, a regimental temperance meeting was held in the barracks... Roberts' quilt, containing 28,000 pieces of cloth, most artistic in design, was exhibited during the meeting. Sir Hope and Lady Grant, who were present, so admired it, that Lady Grant at once gave the soldier £10 for it.

Not just the preserve of women, the relaxing craft of patchwork was popular with men, particularly soldiers, in Victorian times. Here a wounded British soldier concentrates on making a cloth coverlet as a form of occupational therapy. He is probably working with fabric from military uniforms

So virtue was rewarded! Roberts sent his third quilt to *The British Workman* and to encourage such 'self help' the magazine, in the same article, called for a buyer for it. It noted that 'many soldiers devote their leisure time to needlework and other useful employments' and suggested exhibitions should be held of their work.

Sometimes, quilts were made by groups to raise funds for their church or a special charity. People would give a donation to the cause and their name would be embroidered on a patch of the quilt. The finished product might then be sold or given as a present to the minister.

It was popular also to make quilts for hospitals with each square or rectangle bearing an improving text – whether this actually cheered up the patients is not recorded! The texts were either embroidered on to the patches or might be printed. *The British Workman* of November 1876 has an article about a Mr Mimpriss who perfected a technique for 'the printing and engraving of Scripture texts on cloth that would bear washing in cold or hot water without injury'.

Mr Mimpriss actually started work on a quilt made up from this cloth but unfortunately he died before it was completed. A friend, Mr Whitehead, arranged to carry out 'the patchwork quilt work for the benefit of the bed-ridden widow'. He was also 'sending out the sets of texts for which orders were given during Mr Mimpriss' lifetime, and we rejoice that in many homes both aged and juvenile fingers have already made up many very beautiful quilts... We hope that Mr Mimpriss' quilts will soon be found in thousands of homes.' Mr Whitehead was also taking more orders for sets of texts and the magazine had a suggestion to make as to the final destination of finished products. 'The rich should present quilts for the beds of the aged inmates of hospitals, workhouses, almshouses, etc.'

The aim of my book is not quite such an improving one, as I am rather more concerned with the enjoyment of a pleasant and creative hobby than spreading a message. I have chosen some of the most popular types and designs of patchwork of the Victorian era as the basis for a series of projects, from pin cushions, sachets and box tops to a full-sized quilt, many of which are directly inspired by existing nineteenth-century pieces. I hope making them gives you as much pleasure as I have had getting them together.

LOG CABIN

Many people think that Log Cabin is a North American style of patchwork but it has a long tradition on both sides of the Atlantic. One of the oldest known types of patchwork, it was being done in Scotland by at least the middle of the eighteenth century and was popular in Ireland and England in the Victorian era.

The design has been known under a number of different names, including Roof Pattern, Canadian Logwood, Straight Patchwork and even the Mummy Pattern because a nineteenth-century writer thought it looked like the 'swathing bands of mummies'. The most widely-known name, however, is Log Cabin and it is made in a rather different way from most patchwork as the strips which go to make up the pattern are sewn to a foundation fabric, instead of the pieces being joined directly to one another. No template is needed as strips of fabric are made up into a square around a small central square.

The most common colour for the central patch was red with strips of light-coloured fabrics on two adjacent sides and dark colours on the other two sides. This is normally taken to represent the red glow of a fire casting light on one side of a room and causing shadows on the other.

Different fabrics were used for Log Cabin – woollens, silks, satin, velvets, or a mixture of fabrics. Because the patchwork is made by sewing on to a firmly-woven foundation fabric, it is quite possible to mix types and weights of fabric in the same piece of work.

The Victorians often used ribbons so the patchwork was sometimes known as Ribbon patchwork and the central square was quite likely to be embroidered.

When a number of Log Cabin squares have been made they can be arranged in a variety of different

Opposite: This silk coverlet was made in the 1880s by Mary Hannah Mitchelson and her sister Margaret Elizabeth – two prolific Cumbrian needle-women. It is made of 5in (12.5cm) squares, each consisting of 5 strips. The coverlet is particularly effective because one side of each square is black, which creates dramatic crosses against a brightly coloured background. The lace edging is particularly Victorian in style

ways. A popular Victorian arrangement can be seen in the antique Cumbrian quilt on page 13 and on the one below. Here the squares have been assembled in fours with all the light sides together. This means that when the quilt is made up, four dark sides are also together, making a pattern of light crosses on a dark ground and vice versa.

Another common design is that used for the Doll's ribbon quilt on page 18. For this the squares are assembled with the dark corners to one side. This design is known in America as Straight Furrows. An alternative version of the same pattern has been used for the Scrap bag Coverlet (see page 16) by arranging the squares in the same way but changing the size of the squares. A double row of 8in (20cm) squares surrounds a central group of nine 16in (40cm) squares, each of which has a 4in (10cm) Log Cabin square in the centre.

There are numerous other possible arrangements as well as slightly different versions of the basic square. Courthouse (or Capital) Steps is such a design. Here, instead of two adjacent sides of the square being the same colouring, opposite sides are the same. A more complicated version, Pineapple, involves strips across the corners of squares as well as horizontal and vertical ones.

This Log Cabin patchwork coverlet was also made by the Mitchelson sisters and is in warm, woollen fabrics – probably intended as a carriage rug. Although the design is basically the same as the coverlet on page 13, this rug has a different feel about it, not only because of the choice of fabric but also because of the colouring, the number of strips making up a square, and the relatively large size of the central red patch

Opposite: A Victorian magazine illustration shows a mother supervising a small child at work on a log cabin quilt 'It's my thousandth quilt', exclaims the industrious child

SCRAP BAG COVERLET

Victorian women frequently collected scraps of fabric, off-cuts from dressmaking, or good pieces cut from worn-out clothing or remnants. This coverlet is in this tradition, being made largely of manufacturer's samples.

Size

88in (2.2m) square (including borders) The quilt is made up from 64 8in (20cm) squares, 9 16in (40cm) squares and 9 4in (10cm) squares of Log Cabin. Each 16in (40cm) square is created round a 4in (10cm) one. The quilt is bordered with three strips of fabric, 1¼in (31mm), ¾in (18mm) and 2in (5cm) wide.

The method for making up a square of Log Cabin of whatever size is basically the same. The only variations are in the size of the central square and the width and number of the surrounding strips. Log Cabin patchwork can be made up either by hand or by machine. The strips are sewn into place and then the excess is cut off, so the length of the strips is immaterial. The instructions given here are for one 8in (20cm) square.

MATERIALS

White or natural coloured cotton foundation fabric (an old bed sheet is ideal).
Fabric in eight colours – four dark shades, four light ones – pieces at least 9×4in (23×10cm) for the strips.
Small piece of fabric for the central square (buy enough fabric for the centres of all the squares you need to make one article).
Sewing thread.
Seam allowance ¼in (6mm)

ORDER OF WORK

Cut all the fabric on the straight grain. Cut an 8½in (21.5cm) square of foundation fabric. Fold on the diagonals and press to mark the centre (or mark with lines of basting). This will help you to keep a good square when making up the Log Cabin.
Cut the four dark and four light fabrics into 1¼in (31mm) wide strips. Cut a 2¼in (5.7cm) square from the small piece of fabric.
Using the diagonal lines as a guide, pin and baste the square right side up,

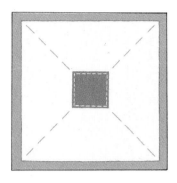

Pin and baste the central square centrally, right side up, on the foundation square

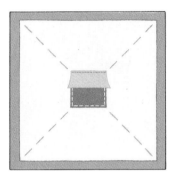

Pin and stitch a paler strip to the square, ¼in (6mm) from the edge

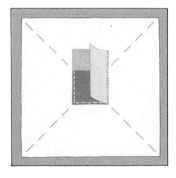

Pin and stitch a second strip along the second side of the square and then over the first strip

centrally on to the foundation square (Fig 1).

Pin and then stitch a light coloured strip to the square, ¼in (6mm) from the edge with right sides together. Cut off the excess fabric (Fig 2). Turn back the strip and press. Pin and stitch a second strip of the same colour along the second side of the square and one short end of the first strip (Fig 3).

Repeat the process on the third and fourth sides of the square, using one of the dark fabrics. Continue with the other six fabrics in the same way, keeping the pale fabrics on one side of

the square and the dark ones on the other.

When the required number of Log Cabin squares have been made up sew them together in strips. Then sew the strips together.

NOTE As you will see from the antique quilts and this modern one, it is not essential for each square to be made from the same selection of fabrics. In fact, this is rarely seen with old examples. What is important is to make the centre of each square from the same fabric as this gives unity to the whole piece of work.

A modern coverlet made in the true patchwork tradition of using rag bag scraps with a variety of floral patterns in shades of maroon and inky blues. The scheme is unified by having all the central squares cut from one fabric and having a triple border. The squares have been arranged in a simple Straight Furrows design

DOLL'S RIBBON QUILT

This miniature bedcover is made from ribbon instead of fabric strips and the technique is slightly different. As there are no raw edges to enclose, the ribbon is top-stitched into place. The centre of each square is the traditional red, with creams and pinks on one side (the light colours) and three shades of blue, from pale to deep turquoise (the dark colours) on the other. In each case the palest of the three colours is placed closest to the centre.

Size
Approximately 11½×15in (29×38cm)

MATERIALS

2¼yds (2.5m) of 1in (2.5cm)-wide red ribbon
1¾yds (1.5m) each of ⅝in (15mm)-wide light cream and pale blue ribbons
2¼yds (2m) each of ⅝in (15mm)-wide cream and mid-turquoise ribbons
3yds (2.5m) each of ⅝in (15mm)-wide pink and deep turquoise ribbons
14×17in (35.5×43cm) piece of cotton foundation fabric
Sewing threads to match ribbons

ORDER OF WORK

The seam allowance on the ribbon strips is ⅛in (3mm) along the selvedge edges. Allow at least ¼in (6mm) on the cut edges as they will fray.
Cut 12 3¾in (9.5cm) squares of foundation fabric, on the straight grain. Mark the diagonals as described for Scrap bag coverlet (page 16).
Cut a piece of red ribbon 1½in (37mm) long (i.e. slightly longer than the width). Pin and baste it to the centre of the foundation square.
Place the cream ribbon, right side up, so that it overlaps one neatened edge of the red ribbon by ⅛in (3mm).

Pin and top-stitch in place with matching thread, making sure the stitches go through both ribbons. Cut off the excess cream ribbon.
Using the same colour and with right side up, pin and top-stitch the next piece of ribbon in place along the second side, overlapping the red ribbon to a greater degree to account for the extra width (i.e. you should finish with a central square). Repeat with the third and fourth sides using the pale blue ribbon.
Continue working around the square with the remaining four colours, using the darkest shades in each group on the outside.
Make up 11 more squares in the same way.
With right sides together, sew the squares together in four strips of three, working ⅛in (3mm) from the edge and with the blue ribbons to the left. Press lightly.
Join the strips together in the same way. Press lightly.
Top-stitch a strip of red ribbon along each short end of the cover. Then top-stitch another strip along each side.
The cover can be lined to make a coverlet or given an interlining as well to make a quilt.

Opposite: Ribbons have been used for this doll-sized bed cover. The design, popular in the nineteenth century, is called Straight Furrows

Left: Make up 12 squares to this colour scheme, using ribbons in 7 different colours

SQUARES AND TRIANGLES

Simple squares and triangles can be arranged in numerous ways to make up a square block for a repeat design. This technique was particularly popular with settlers in the New World. Due to limited space it was simpler to make things that could be done in the lap and it was also possible for a number of people to piece blocks for the same quilt. It was only the making up into a complete top and, more particularly, quilting it, which needed more space. Homesteads were widely scattered and the task of quilting would often be the excuse for a quilting bee, a day-long get-together.

Block patterns are numerous and sometimes very complex and usually have very evocative names. This one is very effective in its freshness and simplicity, but so far as I can find out, has no name. The block is made up of four squares, turned through 45 degrees and framed with triangles to make another square. This square is then turned again with four more triangles used to make the complete square block.

Although patchwork and quilting are usually thought of as feminine occupations, there is a strong tradition of men being involved in both. Samuel Ross was such a man. He was born in the Canadian province of New Brunswick, but became apprenticed to a tailor in Boston, where he gained his sewing skills. He made this quilt with his wife, Matilda Ingram Ross, in the early years of this century. It was sewn by hand from work-shirt and pyjama fabrics, including some early homespun.

The quilt is made up of 36 12in (30cm) squares in checks and stripes. The fabrics vary from block to block, with mostly blues being chosen, plus some reds. The 5in (12.5cm) border is a small-print cotton. The finished patchwork was quilted in two designs. All of it, except the border which has chevrons worked over it, is quilted in a fan pattern

Below: A nineteenth-century painting reveals a delicate patchwork quilt, perhaps made of scraps of dress prints, on an invalid's bed

Opposite: This quilt was made by a husband and wife team, Samuel and Matilda Ross, in the early part of the twentieth century. It was hand-pieced without papers, given a thin interlining and a cotton backing and then quilted

ONE-BLOCK CUSHION

This pattern is interesting enough to be used as a single block on a cushion, workbag or on the top of a stool. Five different checked and striped fabrics have been chosen for the block, with two of them also being used to border the design to create a cushion.

Make up this design using the American method, by hand or with a sewing machine (see page 96).

Size

Block 12in (30cm) square

MATERIALS

Five different, checked and striped cotton fabrics as follows: small piece approximately 8×4in (20×10cm) (this fabric appears only in the central square of the block).

10in (23cm) of 36in (90cm) wide fabric in each of four designs.

Matching thread.

ORDER OF WORK

Templates are finished size. Add ¼in (6mm) seam allowance when cutting out fabric. (See page 95 for making templates.)

Cut 2 of (A) in each of the first two fabrics, on the straight grain. Cut 4 of (B) in a third fabric. Cut 2 of (C) in each of the remaining fabrics.

Following the photograph, make up the block. Start by sewing two of the square patches together. Press. Repeat with the other two squares.

A

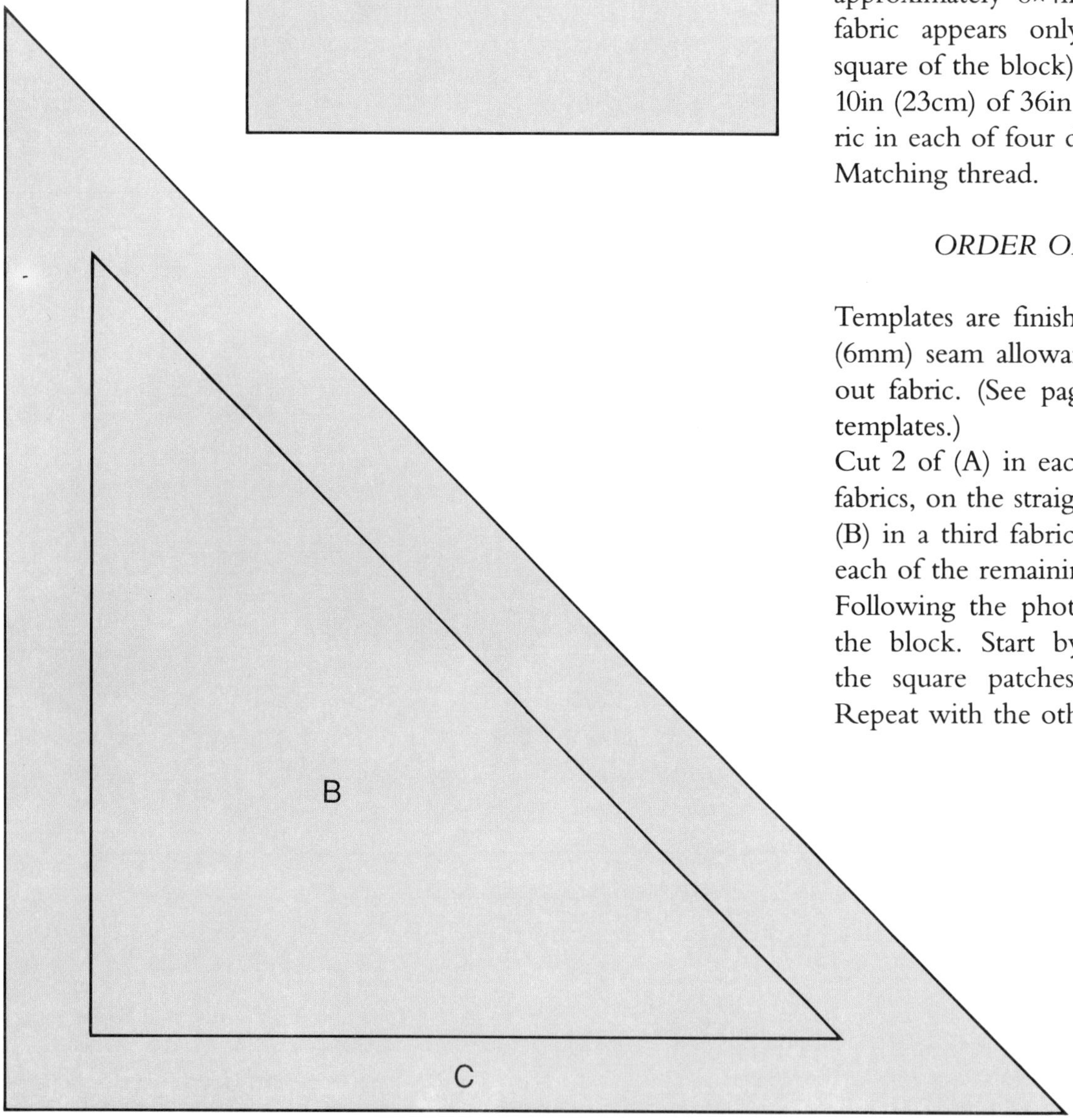

B

C

Join together to make up the central square of the block. Press.

Sew a piece (B) to two opposite sides of the square. Sew the remaining (B) pieces to the other two sides. Press. This makes a larger square.

Repeat with the (C) patches. This completes the block.

NOTE When cutting out right-angled triangles for blocks the rule is to have the sides adjacent to the right angle on the straight grain (see page 92). This rule has been broken here to make use of particular fabric patterns and so the other side of the triangle has been placed on the straight grain.

This cushion, inspired by Samuel and Matilda Ross's quilt on page 21, follows the checks and stripes theme of the original, but the colours are bolder, dramatic reds, greys and black

TUMBLING BLOCKS

The design known as Tumbling Blocks, Baby Blocks or the Box pattern was a favourite on both sides of the Atlantic throughout the nineteenth century. Originally used as an all-over design or border pattern for bedcovers, it was later made up into a variety of domestic furnishings, including cushions, curtains, chair seats and footstools.

It is made from three diamonds which together form a hexagon. When three different fabrics, often a dark, a medium and a light colour, are used, the illusion of a three-dimensional block is created. When repeated over an area the appearance is of a whole stack of blocks rather like children's building bricks. This design was used also as a quilting pattern.

An alternative pattern can be made by using six of the diamonds in a single fabric to form a star. Fabrics might be silk, velvet, cotton or woollen cloth, depending on the object being made and the taste and resources of the maker.

The footstool shown here was made from military uniforms. This fabric was used for a good deal of patchwork in the Victorian era – much of it worked by soldiers. This was not made by a soldier but by a daughter of the regiment. Nellie Bonnett, who came from an Indian Army family, made this stool in the 1880s from the uniforms of officers killed in the Indian Mutiny.

The design has been cleverly worked out to make the most of the dramatic black, red, white, blue and grey colouring. On the top, the box pattern radiates from a central six-point star. The boxes along the top and bottom edges of the stool have two dark sides which make a strong border and the star pattern reappears on the two short edges. The side panels feature diagonal stripes of diamonds with white used to separate and define the strong lines of red and blue.

Above: Tumbling Blocks, a favourite design on both sides of the Atlantic, uses brilliant silks, satins and brocades to create an illusion of a three-dimensional block

Opposite: Nellie Bonnett's footstool, made in the 1880s from soldier's uniforms. The firm, felty wool proved a hard-wearing choice, although now showing signs of age

HEXAGONAL TABLECLOTH

The fact that each box or block of the Tumbling Blocks pattern is a hexagon inspired the shape of this cloth. It is usual to work this design using the English method but it can be worked by the American method if you prefer (see page 96).

Opposite: Silk, satin and velvet was frequently chosen for the Tumbling Blocks pattern and here it is used for a hexagonal-shaped tablecloth in silky fabrics, edged with a Victorian-looking bobble fringe

Size

30in (76cm) diameter; each of the six sides measures 15in (38cm)

MATERIALS

½yd (45cm) of 45in (114cm)-wide silky fabric in each of three colours, blue, black and aubergine
Matching thread
Thin card (for the English method)
3¼yds (3m) of black bobble fringe

ORDER OF WORK

The templates are finished size. Cut papers from thin card. Add ¼in (6mm) seam allowance when cutting out fabric. (See page 95–96 for making templates and cutting papers.)

Using template (A) and with two sides on the straight grain, cut out 44 shapes in each colour.

Using template (B) and with one short side on the straight grain, cut out 8 shapes in each colour. (If the fabric has a pattern, such as a 'watered silk' effect, make sure the design lies in the same direction on each piece.)

Make up the cloth, following the illustration below, using three (A) shapes – one in each colour – for the boxes. Complete the design with (B) shapes as appropriate.

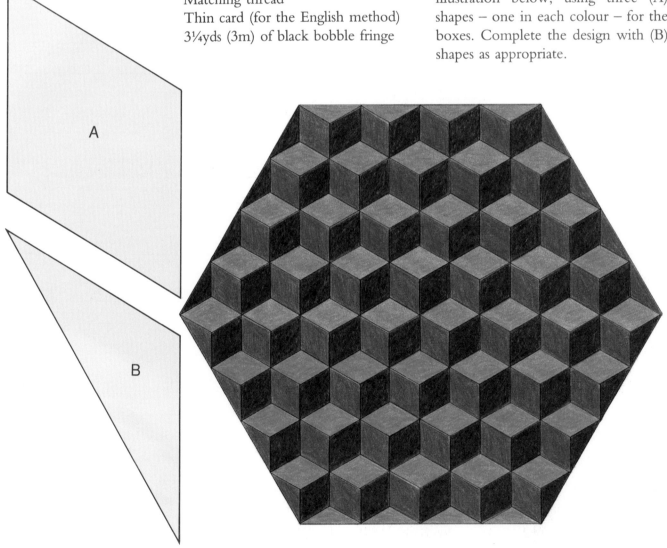

LONG DIAMOND

A shape frequently seen in Victorian patchwork is the long diamond with angles of 45 and 135 degrees. This can be made up into an eight-point star. There are many nineteenth-century quilts which have several hundreds of small long diamonds making up one huge eight-point star as a central motif. In Britain this design is known simply as Star but in North America, where more evocative and romantic names are used for patchwork, it is known as Star of Bethlehem and Lone Star.

The diamond is equally attractive when positioned in a simple lattice pattern. When brightly coloured silk is used the effect is of a stained glass window.

At the beginning of the nineteenth century, small articles in diamond patchwork were often the work of children as the careful stitching needed to work accurate corners was considered good practice for plain sewing. One little girl made a set of velvet antimacassars in diamond pattern 'from ballgowns of the landed gentry'. Velvet would have been a difficult fabric to work, even for an adult, so her achievement is all the more notable. As the century progressed and patchwork became a pastime for the middle and upper classes, ladies addicted to fancy-work made seat covers, footstools, tea cosies, and even trimmed clothing with patchwork. They continued to make warm patchwork quilts and comforters for the poor, however, recycling worn-out clothing, and encouraged the less fortunate to apply themselves to this useful craft.

There is not much call for antimacassars these days – an evening bag made up of small brightly-coloured silk diamonds or a harlequin cushion in different-sized diamonds of silky fabrics might be rather more useful, and attractive things to make from patchwork.

The star motif was considered a symbol of good luck and fertility in the north of England, where this quilt was made around 1870. The huge central star of long diamonds and the smaller stars spinning from it were appliquéd to the background fabric by sewing machine although the quilting is worked by hand

EVENING BAG

The bag is made from long diamonds in six jewel colours, framed with black velvet to add impact to the design. To help give the silk stability and to emphasize the shapes, the work has been quilted along the seams. Work long diamonds using the English method (see page 96).

Size
Patchwork measures approximately 5¼in×6¾in (13.3×17cm)

MATERIALS

Scraps of silk in six colours
Matching threads
Thin card

ORDER OF WORK

Templates are finished size. Cut papers from thin card. Add ¼in (6mm) seam allowance when cutting out fabric. (See pages 95–96 for making templates and cutting papers.)
Using template (A), cut out 5 red, 4 pink, 3 green, 2 blue, 2 gold and 2 maroon pieces, with two sides on the straight grain.
Using template (B), cut out 1 red, 1 pink, 1 blue and 1 gold piece, with one short side on the straight grain.
Using template (C), cut out 2 green, 3 blue, 2 gold and 2 maroon pieces, with one long side on the straight grain.
Using template (D), cut out 1 green and 1 maroon piece, with the longest side on the straight grain.
Make up following the pattern.

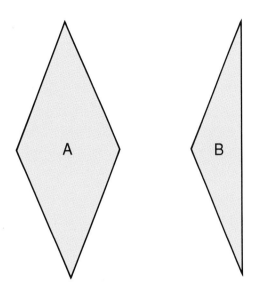

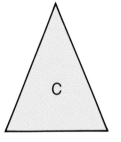

Opposite: The bright jewel colours used for this drawstring evening bag are enhanced by the 'frame' of black velvet. In true Victorian tradition, the bag is made from scraps of fabric

Follow the diagram below to assemble the diamonds and triangles for the evening bag

HARLEQUIN CUSHION

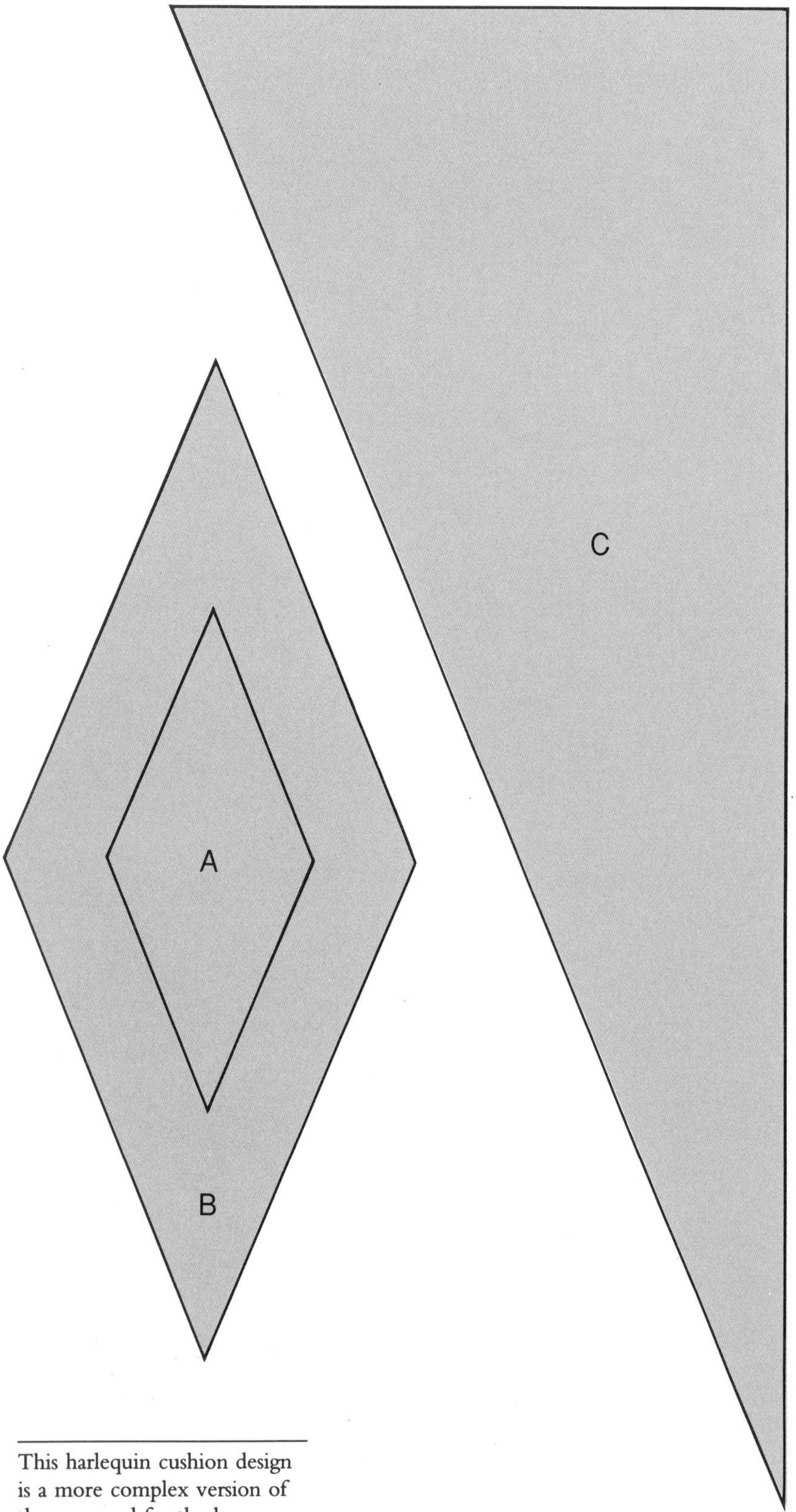

Four different coloured silk fabrics have been used to make up this design. It consists entirely of long diamonds in a progression of sizes. The centre of the pattern is four small diamonds, sewn together to make a larger diamond. This central diamond is then surrounded by eight more of the same size, making a nine-patch long diamond. The panel is completed with four triangles which together make up into a long diamond, again nine times bigger than the one just completed. As for the Evening bag, use the English method (see page 96).

Size

Patchwork measures approximately 8×15in (20×38cm)

MATERIALS

8in (20cm) square each of four different colours of silk
16in (40cm) square each of two of the colours (to complete a 15in (38cm) square cushion)

ORDER OF WORK

Templates given here, two diamonds and a right-angled triangle, are finished size. Cut papers from thin card. Add ¼in (6mm) seam allowance when cutting out fabric.

Using template (A), cut out 1 piece in each of the four colours, with two sides of the diamond on the straight grain.

Using template (E), cut out 2 pieces in each colour, with two sides of the diamond on the straight grain.

Using template (F), cut out 1 piece in each colour, with the sides adjacent to the right angle on the straight grain. Make up the patchwork following the photograph opposite.

This harlequin cushion design is a more complex version of the one used for the bag on page 30. Only four colours have been used

CRAZY PATCHWORK

Opposite: Crazy patchwork coverlet made from velvet, silk and satin in striking shades. Made in about 1880, the pieces are overstitched with herringbone in a contrasting colour

Above: Patchwork quilts, unbeatable for warmth, were particularly popular in the Victorian nursery

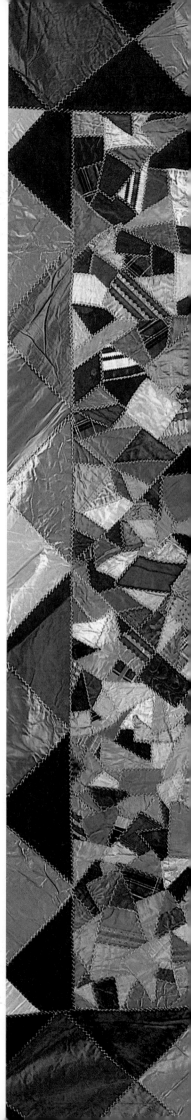

This type of patchwork has characteristics in common with Log Cabin in that no papers or templates are used and the patches are sewn on to a foundation fabric. Here the resemblance ends. With Crazy patchwork, there is no careful measuring and squaring up of pieces. Random shapes are stitched to the foundation fabric in any arrangement according to the whim of the maker.

The first patch is sewn to the foundation with running stitch worked all round the edge, the next is laid down with the adjacent edge overlapping it and then sewn down in the same way. This process continues until the whole surface is covered. The joins are then covered with embroidery.

This style of work was much loved by ladies in the late-Victorian era who made a whole variety of items in Crazy patchwork to decorate their parlours. The style fitted in perfectly with the pre-vailing passion for fancy-work. Fabrics would be off-cuts from dressmaking – silks, satins, velvets and brocades – with the joins covered in a variety of different stitches, from simple herring-bone and feather stitch and intricate stitches seldom seen today.

Never content to leave a good thing alone, these enthusiastic women frequently went on to add beads and more embroidery to the patches. This is not a hardwearing type of work and, considering the vast amount of it made, little nineteenth-century Crazy patchwork is still intact. It is a very attractive technique for making small articles not intended for heavy use and which won't need frequent washing. A very Victorian choice would be a padded tea cosy.

The lady's evening waistcoat on page 39 is a vari-ation on Crazy patchwork. In this case, larger, straight-sided pieces of cloth have been machine-stitched on to a foundation fabric.

TEA COSY

The cosy is made from a mixture of silks, satins, damask and velvet in different colours. The joins are covered with herring-bone stitch worked in black embroidery thread.

Size
12½in×9½in (31.2×24cm)

MATERIALS

An assortment of fabrics in different colours and textures
Matching threads
Black Coton à broder no. 16 (or stranded embroidery thread)
14×11in (35×28cm) cotton sheeting or a similar fabric. (You will need two pieces of fabric if the back and front of the cosy are to be in patchwork)

ORDER OF WORK

Make up the patchwork on a larger piece of foundation fabric than the finished article as it might 'shrink' or warp as you sew.

Take the first patch and trim it to a convenient shape, cutting off any frayed edges. Pin to one edge of the cotton foundation fabric. Using matching thread, sew in place with small running stitches (Fig 1).

Take the next patch and trim as before. Turn under ⅛in (3mm) on one raw edge. Lay this second patch next to the first, with the turned-in edge overlapping it by ¼in (6mm). Pin and stitch in place (Fig 2). Repeat until the whole surface is covered.

Using Coton à broder or three strands of stranded embroidery thread, work herring-bone stitch (or an embroidery stitch of your choice) over the joins to cover the running stitches.

NOTE It is advisable to turn under raw edges before sewing them in place to prevent fraying. Patches may also be ironed to a very lightweight iron-on interfacing. Some fabrics, such as velvet, are not suitable for either treatment; in this case, make sure all raw edges of such patches are covered by another patch.

Pin the first patch to the edge of the foundation fabric, sew in places with small running stitches

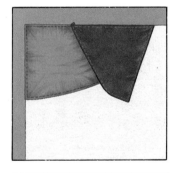

Turn in the edge on the second patch and, overlapping by ¼in (6mm), sew to the first patch

Right: Detail of the tea cosy, showing embroidery stitches worked over the joins

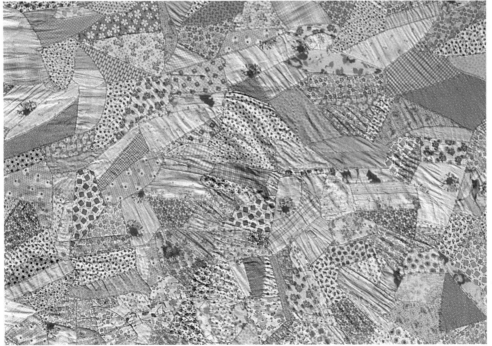

Above: Tea cosies are still in daily use in parts of England, especially in rural districts. Often made as fancy needlework projects, they are also treasured as collectors' items.

Left: This Crazy patchwork coverlet, made around 1880, incorporates many different sizes and shapes of fabric in pastels and mini-prints to create a pleasing effect, suitable for use in a nursery, perhaps

EVENING WAISTCOAT

This waistcoat is cut from a piece of patchwork made from several black fabrics of different textures. These were cut into strips of varying widths and were joined together to make a completely new and unique cloth. To add further interest, folded squares of Somerset patchwork were inserted between two of the strips (see page 83).

The fabric was then cut up into different sized triangles. The patterns for the waistcoat fronts and back were marked out with basting thread on a foundation fabric. The triangles were then machine-stitched on to the foundation fabric – rather like a crazy form of Log Cabin. When the patch-work was completed the pattern pieces were cut out to size.

The shape is very simple and un-fitted. There are no facings, instead the waistcoat is lined and the raw edges bound. There are no side and shoulder seams; instead the back and fronts are held together with covered buttons and loops.

To make a similar waistcoat to fit an average size you will need to make up a piece of fabric 18in (45cm) wide by 36in (90cm) long. Note that the piece of patchwork you make should be long and narrow rather than wide and short. You will also need to choose a basic waistcoat pattern of a simple shape and without darts.

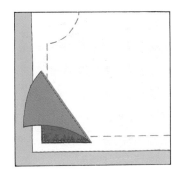

Mark the waistcoat pieces on the foundation fabric with basting thread

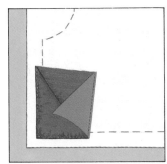

Machine-stitch the patches on the foundation fabric, then cut the pattern pieces to size

Patchwork lends itself to clothing as well as home furnishings, as this Victorian Christmas card shows

Opposite: For this elegant waistcoat, a specially made-up fabric has been cut up and reassembled to give a fascinating pattern of light and shade

GRANDMOTHER'S FAN

A wide variety of different block patterns are based on the fan shape, such as Friendship Fan, Fanny's Fan and Imperial Fan. Probably the best known is the one featured on this delightful nineteenth-century piece, Grandmother's Fan.

Although most of the patchwork and quilting done in the nineteenth century was made up into bed covers, there were also a lot of table covers, carriage rugs and throws made. This piece (right) is a throw and would probably have been used on a sofa or draped over a piano. It was made in the early 1880s by a Pennsylvania Dutch (Deutsch) woman, Ellen Rimert of Northumberland County, Pennsylvania, USA.

The throw was made by hand, with all the pieces being cut without a template and some of the squares are not true. Once the top had been pieced, Ellen appears to have gone to town with the embroidery, outlining every seam, using a whole variety of stitches, including flag stitch, variegated coral, picot and feather stitches. At first glance the design looks more like an example of Crazy patchwork than Grandmother's Fan.

The top is fine wool chalice and the backing is cotton satin with a filling between the two layers. The quilting is purely utilitarian, serving just to hold the three layers together, with the stitching outlining the outer edge of each fan and square block. The throw, like many pieces of the time, is edged with a frill.

The fan blocks for the throw are assembled in fours, with two diagonally opposite ones placed together and the other two reversed. Like a great many block patterns, however, a single Grandmother's Fan block can stand alone. On page 43, one block has been used for the front of a workbag. Trace-off templates are given to work the patchwork.

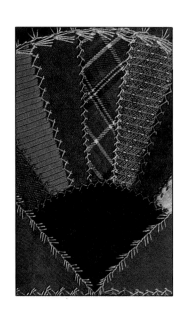

This throw was made entirely by hand, the pieces having been cut out without using templates thus the fans vary slightly in size.

WORK BAG

Soft, dress weight wool/cotton mixture fabrics in warm, rich colours have been chosen to give this bag a period feel, but you can use cotton fabrics if you prefer.

Make up this design using the American method, by hand or with a sewing machine (see page 96). Strips of plain fabric were added to the sides. (The amounts of fabric given will make up two sides of the bag.)

Size

Block measures 11½in (29cm) square.

MATERIALS

Wool/cotton mixture fabrics in the following colours and amounts:

¼yd (23cm) of 45in (114cm) wide plain dark red

¼yd (23cm) of 45in (114cm) wide plain dark green

7×12½in (18×32cm) dark red patterned fabric

6½×3in (16.5×7.5cm) navy patterned fabric

6½×3in (16.5×7.5cm) purple patterned fabric

6½×3in (16.5×7.5cm) green patterned fabric

Matching thread

ORDER OF WORK

Templates are finished size. Add ¼in (6mm) seam allowance when cutting fabric, placing one straight edge of each template on the straight grain.

Using template (A) cut out pieces in patterned fabrics as follows: 4 red, 1 navy, 1 purple, 1 green.

Using template (B), cut 1 plain red.

Using template (C), cut 1 plain red. Reverse the template and cut 1 plain green. (This gives two mirror image corner sections.)

Make up the block, following the photograph. Sew the pieces (A) of the fan together and press. Then sew the completed fan shape to piece (B) and press. Sew the two corner (C) sections together and press. Sew the outer edge of the fan to the corner section. Press.

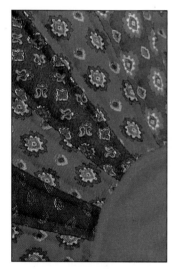

Opposite: Fabrics in rich, warm colourings and traditional patterns give a period feel to this modern workbag. Unlike the throw on page 41, the pieces of the block have been outlined with quilting rather than with embroidery stitches

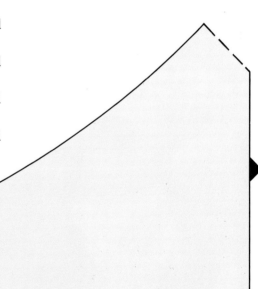

C

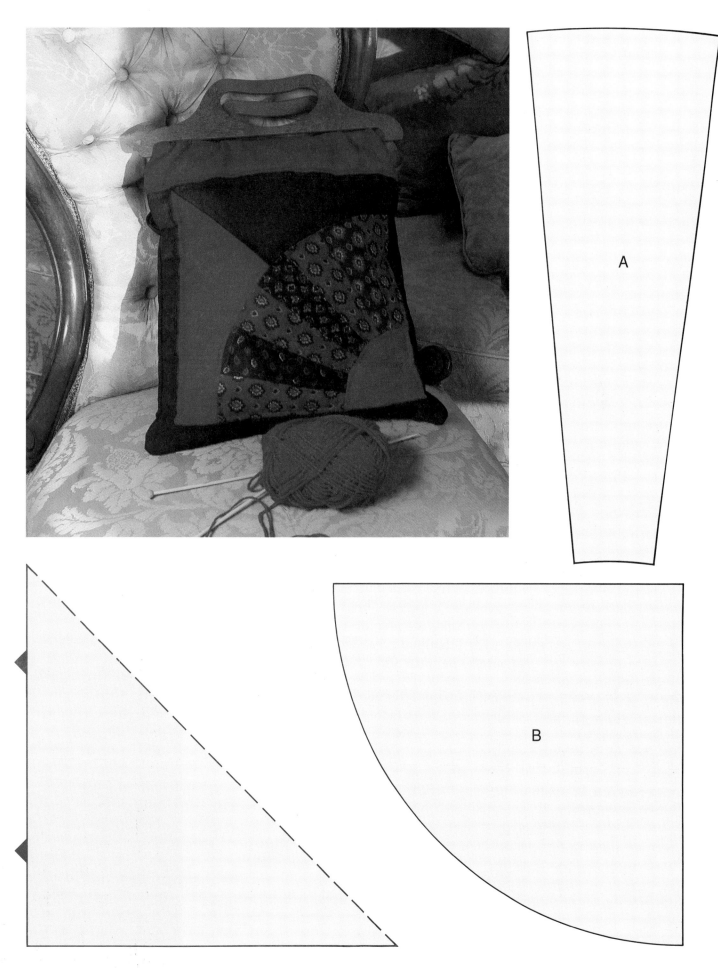

EIGHT-POINT STAR

This Eight-point Star pattern is really two stars – one superimposed on the other, made up into a square block. The design features, as a large central motif surrounded by plain borders, on a number of north of England quilts. The simple and bold colouring – pink and white, red and white, blue and white – gives maximum impact and shows off quilting to great advantage.

In the last century there were numerous women in the north of England who quilted for a living, and some who marked out the quilting pattern on quilt tops for others to work. The most famous was quilt 'stamper' Elizabeth Sanderson of Allenheads, Northumberland, who began her working life in the 1890s and continued until her death in the 1930s. This district was noted for its quilting designs and Miss Sanderson's quilt tops, and those of other local stampers, were sold through co-operative shops (jointly owned by many members – in this case local customers – who shared any profits) and by travelling salesmen over a wide area.

The Eight-point Star design, however, does not need to be quilted to be successful.

Opposite: The plain colours and simplicity of the Eight-point Star (detail on right) gave ample scope for the creative flair of the stamper and the expertise of the quilter. A popular patchwork design in Victorian times, a number of such quilts survive in varying colour schemes

EIGHT-POINT STAR STOOL

Firmly-woven lightweight furnishing cotton in two, clear, colours has a timeless effect. Work the design by hand using the American method (see page 96).

Size

Block measures 15¾in (40cm) square
Diameter of top of stool is approximately 17in (43cm)

MATERIALS

¼yd (23cm) of 48in (122cm)-wide cotton fabric, in yellow
¼yd (23cm) of 48in (122cm)-wide cotton fabric, in pale grey
NOTE To complete a footstool with a piped edge you will need ½yd (45cm) of yellow fabric and 1yd (90cm) of grey.
Matching thread

The star-within-a-star design works best as a single image on a piece of work, whether on a full-sized quilt like the one on page 45, a cushion, or on a footstool. Yellow has been teamed with grey here, instead of the traditional white

ORDER OF WORK

Templates on the opposite page, A, B, C, Ci and D, are finished size. Add ¼in (6mm) seam allowance when cutting fabric, placing one edge of each template on the straight grain. Use templates (C) and (D) for a square block; use template (Ci) for a round stool top or cushion. (See page 95 for making templates.)
Using template (A) cut out 8 grey pieces.
Using template (B) cut out 8 yellow pieces.
Using (C) cut out 4 grey pieces.
Using (D) cut out 4 grey pieces.
Or using (Ci) instead of (C) and (D) cut out 8 grey pieces.
Following the photograph below for the complete block, make up the patchwork.

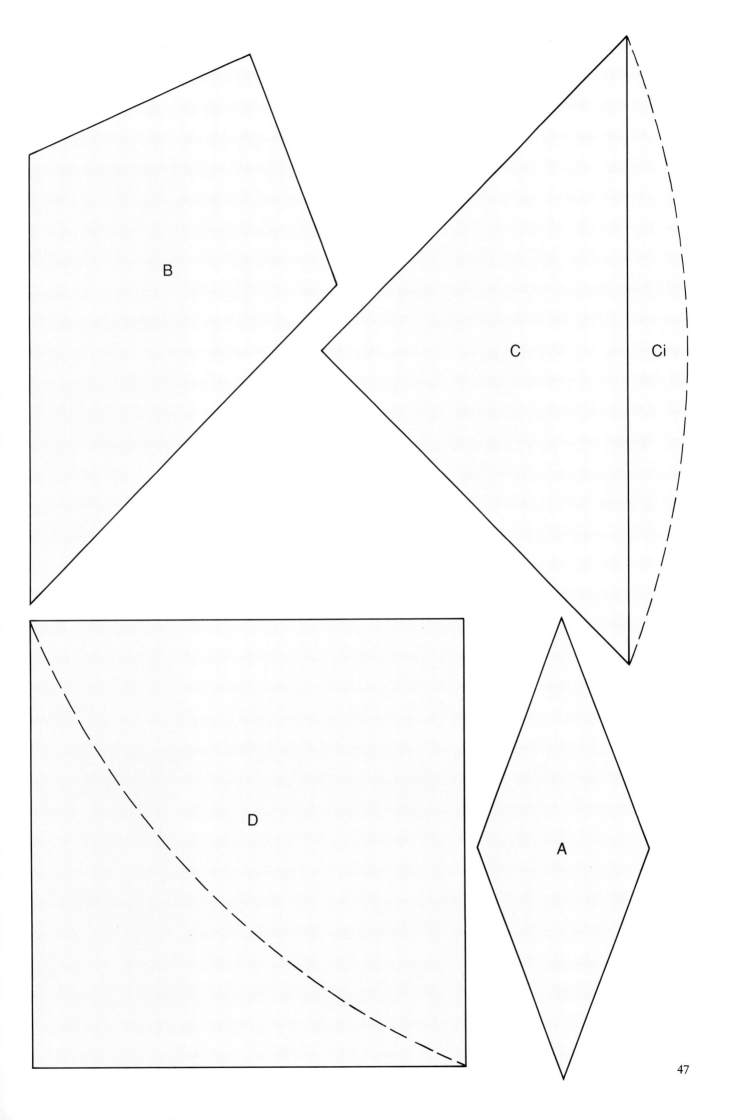

B

C

Ci

D

A

47

NINE-PATCH

Patchwork was originally developed when money and fabric were scarce, and every last scrap had to be used (and reused) to the best advantage. A quilt made today from rag-bag scraps would fit into this tradition of thrift and the simplest way to create it is to sew squares of fabric together until you have made up a large enough piece of cloth for the purpose in mind.

This very simple shape, however, has been used to create a whole range of interesting patterns. One way is to arrange squares in two colours, to give a cross of one colour on a background of another – the design is called Nine-Patch in the United States. Alternatively, three colours can be used, with the third being used as the centre of the cross.

The quilt on the right is based on this arrangement, but the squares have been arranged to give diagonal crosses. The pattern has then been extended to give a double border around the crosses. This quilt was made at the turn of the century from carefully-chosen remnants of flannels and suiting by Sybil Heslop, a farmer's wife from Northumberland in the north of England.

The frilled crib quilt on pages 50–52, made recently for a much-loved granddaughter, uses the same basic Nine-Patch cross design. This time, however, the squares are the conventional way up, making upright crosses.

Another way to arrange blocks of Nine-Patch is to alternate them with blocks of one of the colours to make a simple version of the design known as Irish Chain. The quilt on page 53 is another version of this pattern in which the block is made up of a central square surrounded by four rectangles and four smaller squares. The quilt was made in the latter part of the last century by a Cumbrian woman, Ada Elizabeth Robinson, and is still being used by a descendant today.

Opposite: The basic design of this turn-of-the-century quilt is a repeat pattern of diagonal crosses, each bordered with a different colour, with the whole design outlined with black. The design is symmetrical, based around a central upright cross

CRIB QUILT IN SQUARES

The design is of 12 blocks of nine small squares each, bordered with narrow strips to make larger squares which are in turn separated by narrow strips. The quilt is bordered with more strips and edged with broderie anglaise. It is decorated with embroidery. Make up this design using the American method (see page 96).

Size
The finished quilt measures approximately 21in×29in (55×77cm), plus frill

MATERIALS

The following amounts of 36in (90cm)- wide fabrics:
½yd (45cm) of pink, all-over mini-print (P1)
½yd (45cm) of blue, all-over mini-print (B1)
⅛yd (11.5cm) of paler pink all-over mini-print (P2)
⅛yd (11.5cm) of paler blue all-over mini-print (B2)
⅛yd (11.5cm) each of 4 different floral mini-prints (M1, M2, M4, M5)
¼yd (23cm), of two more floral mini-print (M3, M6)
⅛yd (11.5cm) of rabbit print (B3)
4yd (3.6m) of 1¾in (4.5cm)-wide broderie anglaise
Matching thread
Pink and blue stranded embroidery thread.

ORDER OF WORK

No templates are given for this design as it is made up entirely of squares and strips. The squares are 1½in (4cm) and you should make templates to this size. Add ¼in (6mm) seam allowance when cutting fabric (see page 95).

This delicately patterned quilt, in a variety of prints, with its recurring cross motif, is composed of small squares which together form a nine-patch block. The quilt is traditionally Victorian in style.

A seam allowance of ¼in (6mm) is included on the strips.

Using the template, cut out the following squares with all sides on the straight grain: B2, 24; P2, 24; M1, 12; M2, 12; M3, 12; M4, 12; B3, 12.

Following the single block diagram, and using B2, B3, M1 and M2, join the first nine squares together to make a mainly blue block. Press.

Make up five more blocks in the same way.

Outline each centre square with chain stitch using two strands of stranded embroidery thread.

Repeat with P2, B3, M3 and M4 to make six mainly pink blocks.

Cut the following from fabric P1: 12 strips 1¼×5in (31mm×13.2cm); 12 strips 1¼×6½in (31mm×17cm).

Sew one of the shorter strips to the top, and another to the bottom, of one of the pink blocks. Press. Sew a longer strip to each of the other two sides. Press.

Using two strands of stranded embroidery thread, work feather stitch (see page 105) over the join to outline the Nine-Patch block Repeat with the other five pink blocks.

Cut the same number and size of strips from fabric B1 and repeat the process with the blue blocks.

Cut 15 6½×1¼in (17×31mm) strips from M5.

Following the whole quilt diagram, make up three bands of four squares with lattice strips between the squares and at each end. Press.

Cut four strips of M3, 28¼×1¼in (74×31cm) wide. Join the bands together using these lattice strips. Sew another strip down each long side. From M6, cut 2 strips 21½×1¼in (56.2cm×31mm) and 2 strips 29¾×1¼in (79cm×31mm). Sew the two shorter strips along the top and bottom. Press. Then sew the two longer ones to the sides. Press.

If you wish, add chain stitch crosses in pink or blue, using two strands of stranded embroidery thread, at the corners of borders and intersections of lattice strips.

Make up into a quilt and trim with broderie anglaise.

Below: Follow the top diagram to construct the pink blocks. The lower diagram shows the arrangement for the blue blocks. The diagram to the right shows the complete quilt layout

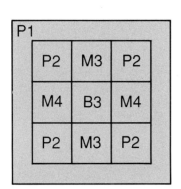

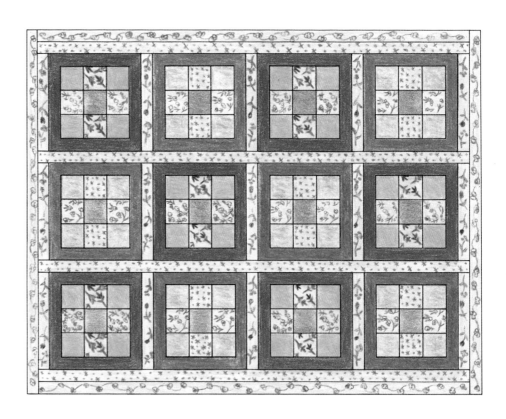

This is one of the many versions of the Irish Chain pattern which appears on quilts on both sides of the Atlantic. It is also known as Puss in the Corner. This quilt, from Cumbria in the north of England, is made from two cotton fabrics, a pink all-over print and a white and blue print. The design is made from 7in (18cm) blocks of 5 pink squares and 4 white rectangles, arranged like a checkerboard with 7in (18cm) squares. The quilt is bordered in pink fabric, diamond quilted.

HEXAGONS

The hexagon is the most common shape in English patchwork and has been popular since at least the beginning of the eighteenth century. This shape is always worked over papers and in the past these were often cut from old letters or newspapers. In some unfinished pieces the papers are still in place, giving fascinating clues to the maker and the date of the work.

There are a variety of different types of hexagons. All have six sides, of course, but the length of these sides and the angles between them are not necessarily equal and they can be joined together to make a whole range of patterns.

The most usual shape, however, is the honeycomb with all sides and angles equal, and the commonest way in which they are sewn together is in groups of seven to make rosettes. The rosettes are frequently made up into an all-over pattern with rows of hexagons in a single colour separating them. This design is sometimes called Grandmother's Flower garden, particularly in America, because the rosettes are said to represent flowers and the surrounding plain hexagons, the garden paths.

This much used shape is sometimes dismissed as boring and ordinary, but it is one of the most interesting and versatile of all. By using the basic honeycomb shape some wonderful patterns have been created. Instead of rosettes, nine patches – arranged in rows of one, two, three, two, one – make a diamond shape. By increasing the number of patches in a row, you can make larger and larger diamonds. Six of the diamonds can be used together to make a star. As with all patchwork, the choice and arrangement of fabrics and colours is an intrinsic part of the design.

In the Victorian era it was fashionable to work with very tiny hexagons, often using silks, velvets

Like many examples of old patchwork, this piece was never completed. Although it is bed-sized, it has remained unlined. The hexagons have been made up into a version of Grandmother's Flower Garden, but instead of rosettes of 7 hexagons at the centre, there are 4. This central group is surrounded by 2 rows of patterned fabric and then the white 'path'

and brocades. The City of Dundee Museum and Art Galleries has a jewel-like hexagonal cloth worked by Mrs Anne Loney which is made from honeycomb-shaped scraps of these luxurious materials.

Although Victorian ladies with time on their hands might make up all sorts of articles, some useful, others rather eccentric, as with all patchwork at this time, the majority of the work would have been made up into bed covers. Rosettes were also frequently made up in combination with diamonds and triangles. The red and white cotton quilt on page 57 is in this pattern and inspired the basket cover on page 62.

As well as being made up into an all-over pattern, hexagons can also be made up into groups, such as rosettes, and appliquéd to another fabric.

Another attractive hexagonal shape is the long hexagon – with two opposite sides longer than the other four. This church window hexagon can be used on its own, but works particularly well when combined with a square. A design made from church windows and squares was chosen for the inner lid of the workbox on page 64.

Opposite: Turkey Red and white was a popular colour scheme for quilts and coverlets in the second half of the, nineteenth century, in Wales, Ireland, in the Isle of Man as well as in the north of England, where this quilt was made. These hexagons are made up in a rather unusual way, which involves a larger shape being stitched on top of a smaller one. The extra fabric along the edges is eased in as the two are sewn together and the loose fabric in the middle is then stitched to give a quilted look

Right: This American nineteenth-century painting shows a quilting party in Pennsylvania. These occasions were often the cue for fun and games in Victorian times, with all the family, from the children up, taking part

GRANDMOTHER'S FLOWER GARDEN BOX TOP

Tiny hexagons in printed cotton have been chosen to cover the top of a box. When cutting the shapes from the floral fabric, window templates were carefully positioned so that one tiny flower was centred on each patch.

Size

Patchwork measures 9in (23cm) square

MATERIALS

⅛yd (11.5cm) of 36in (90cm)-wide floral-patterned fine cotton dress fabric
⅛yd (11.5cm) of 36in (90cm)-wide plain, fine cotton dress fabric
Thin card
Matching thread

ORDER OF WORK

Templates are finished size. Cut papers from thin card. Add ¼in (6mm) seam allowance when cutting fabric, placing two edges of each whole hexagon on the straight grain. (See page 95 for making templates.)

Using template (A), cut out 52 pieces in floral fabric, centring each patch on a flower motif; cut out 53 pieces in plain fabric.
Using template (B), cut out 4 pieces in floral fabric; cut 6 pieces in plain fabric.
Using template (C), cut out 4 pieces in floral fabric; cut 14 pieces in plain fabric.
Using template (D), cut out 4 pieces in floral fabric.
Make up the patchwork following the pattern.

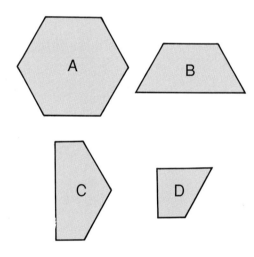

Opposite: This box lid is covered with ½in (12mm) hexagons arranged in the Grandmother's Flower Garden pattern. A Victorian girl might well have made herself a prayerbook cover in this design but using even smaller patches, cut from silk or velvet

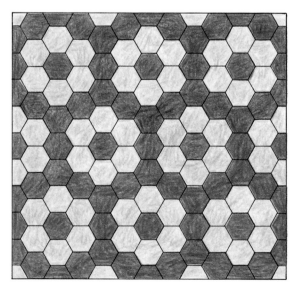

ROSE CUSHION

A rosette of seven patches has been cut from a rose-patterned cotton print and reassembled to make a new design. The whole rosette was then appliquéd to a plain background fabric. The central patch is a single rose; the surrounding ones are cut from the same leafy motif, each patch including also an outer section of a rose.

Size

The rosette is 6½in (16.5cm) in diameter

MATERIALS

Approximately ¼yd (23cm) of 48in (122cm)-wide rose-patterned cotton furnishing fabric (you will need at least this amount to get a sufficient quantity of the same leaf motif).
Matching thread

ORDER OF WORK

The template is finished size. Cut papers from thin card. Add ¼in (6mm) seam allowance when cutting out fabrics. (See page 95 for making templates.)
Using template (E), cut out one rose motif and six leafy ones to make up into a pleasing 'flower'.
Make up a rosette and press. Remove the papers carefully and then press again. Appliqué the rosette to the background fabric (see page 103).

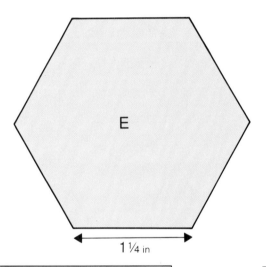

1 ¼ in

Opposite: The patches which make up the rosette on this cushion were cut from a floral fabric. One complete rose and six leaf motifs were rearranged to form the new design

BLUE AND YELLOW BASKET COVER

The pattern for this piece of work was taken from the red and white quilt on page 57. The scale has been changed to suit the size of the basket top. The finished patchwork is edged with a pleated frill of blue cotton. The piece is lined with the same fabric and has a thin wadding between the layers.

Size
Patchwork is 11½in (29cm) in diameter.

MATERIALS

¼yd (23cm) of 48in (122cm)-wide, finely woven furnishing cotton in yellow
¼yd (23cm) of 48in (122cm)-wide, finely woven furnishing cotton in light navy. (Double the quantity to include the frill and lining.)
Matching thread

ORDER OF WORK

Templates are finished size. Cut papers from thin card. Add ¼in (6mm) seam allowance when cutting out fabric. (See page 95 for making templates.)
Using template (F), cut out the following, with two sides on the straight grain: 48 yellow pieces, 7 navy.
Using template (G), cut out 24 navy, with two sides on the straight grain.
Using template (H), cut out 12 navy, with one side on the straight grain.
You also will need to cut out parts of shapes to complete a circle.
Make up the patchwork following the photograph.

Opposite: The red and white quilt on page 57 was the inspiration for this workbasket cover but the scale has been changed to suit the subject. A yellow and navy colour scheme is used here and the patchwork is made up by using the conventional English method (see page 95)

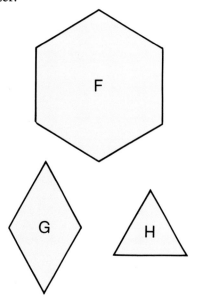

SILK WORKBOX LID

This design, reminiscent of Victorian tiled floors, is created from church window hexagons and squares. A printed silk with a small all-over pattern was used for the hexagons, with the squares in plain, grey silk. The patchwork was quilted to give definition to the design.

Size

Finished size of patchwork, 8⅛in (20.5cm) diameter

MATERIALS

12in (30cm) square scrap of patterned silk
6in (15cm) square scrap of plain silk
Matching thread

ORDER OF WORK

Templates are finished size. Cut papers from thin card. Add ¼in (6mm) seam allowance when cutting out fabric.
Using template (I), cut out 32 patterned pieces with long sides on the straight grain.

Using template (J), cut out 12 plain pieces on the straight grain.
Using template (K), cut out 4 patterned pieces, with two short sides on the straight grain.
Using template (L), cut out 4 patterned pieces, with the long side on the straight grain.
Following the photograph, make up the patchwork.

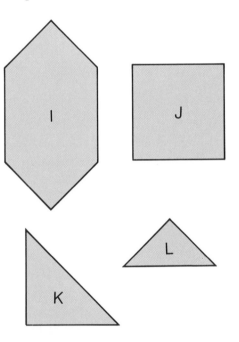

Opposite: The inner lids of this Victorian workbox were lost so new ones were made from a silk scarf and scraps of plain silk. The central lid is made up in a tile design of church window shapes and squares. The outer patches were cut from the border of the silk scarf

FLOWER BASKET

Basket patterns were very popular in both Britain and America and there are dozens of different designs. They might be pieced or appliqué patterns or, as on the quilt opposite, combine the two techniques. The block is basically a pieced design, with the top half being composed of one large triangle with the basket handle appliquéd on to it.

This quilt, which dates from the early part of the twentieth century, was pieced and stamped by the prolific Elizabeth Sanderson of Allenheads, but sewn by Mrs Deborah Adamson of Weardale. The alternate plain white blocks and wide pink border really show up the lovely quilting patterns for which Miss Sanderson was noted.

The cushion design was based on a single block of the quilt, with outer triangles added to complete an upright square shape. Although the design is faithful to the original, using a busy all-over floral print for the basket and outer corners of the cushion has created a rather different effect.

Right: Flower basket quilt in Turkey Red and white, made in about 1880. This pattern was often used on wedding quilts to symbolize prosperity and happiness

Opposite: A pink and white cotton quilt pieced, stamped and quilted in the north of England in the early twentieth century. The quilting was worked by a woman from Weardale, county Durham, and the border design is Weardale Chain, typical of the region

FLOWER BASKET CUSHION

Cotton dress-weight fabrics – a bold all-over design of pink roses on a black background and one picking out a paler shade of pink – were used for this cushion. It is important to have the same part of the design on each triangular patch of the basket, i.e., the same rose in every case, by using a window template (see page 95), and to have the pattern running the same way on all the basket sections.

Make up the design using the American method (see page 96).
NOTE This is one of those occasions when, because of the choice of a particular patterned fabric, you may want to break the rule regarding which side, or sides, of the shapes are on the straight grain.

Size
Cushion measures approximately 15in (37.5cm) square.

MATERIALS

½yd (45cm) of 36in (90cm)-wide dress-weight floral cotton fabric (depending on the pattern you might be able to manage with less fabric).

½yd (45cm) of 36in (90cm)-wide dress-weight plain cotton fabric (this will give enough fabric for the back of the cushion).
Matching thread

ORDER OF WORK

Templates are finished size. Add ¼in (6mm) seam allowance when cutting out fabric. (See page 00 for making templates.)
Using template (A) cut out the following, with the short sides on the straight grain: 9 patterned pieces, 6 plain pieces.
Using template (B), cut 1 patterned piece with the short sides on the straight grain.
Using template (C), cut 1 plain piece with the long sides on the straight grain. Reverse the template and cut a mirror image piece.
Using template (D), cut 1 plain piece with the short sides on the straight grain.
Using template (E), cut 1 plain piece with the short sides on the straight grain.
Using template (F), cut 4 patterned pieces with two short sides on the straight grain.
Using template (G), cut 1 patterned piece with the pattern running the same way as on the rest of the basket.
Make up the patchwork following the pattern.
Appliqué the basket handle (G) on to piece (E), leaving the edges raw at the base of the handle. Then make up the lower half of the basket block, using (A), (B), (C) and (D) pieces. Sew the two halves together. This completes the basket block. Next add two (F) shapes to opposite sides of the square block just made, then add the other two (F) shapes.

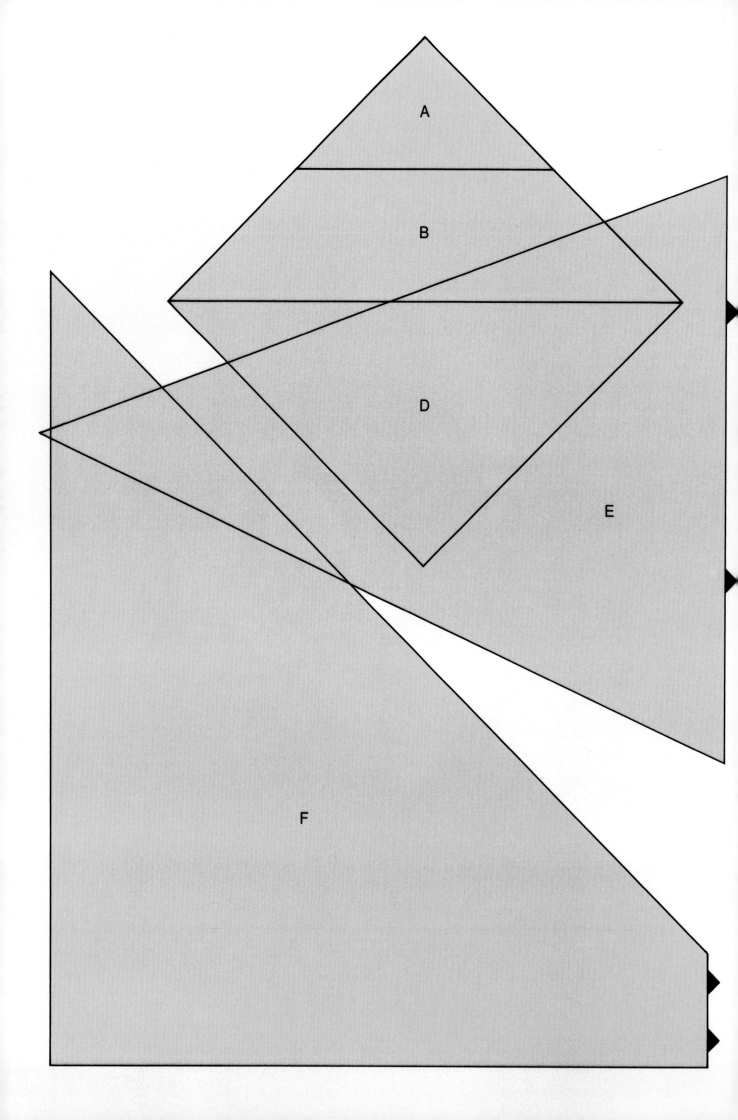

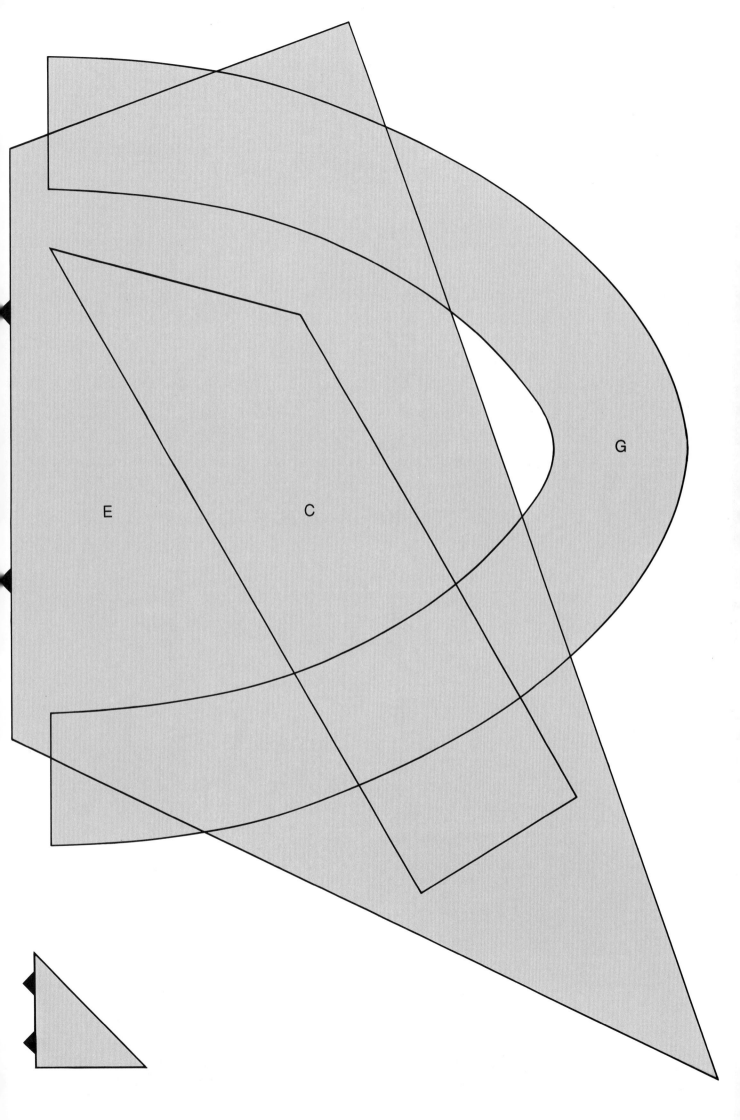

MEDALLION PATCHWORK

Many quilts are finished with a border of some sort, but in a medallion quilt the borders are an intrinsic part of the design. These quilts consist of a central panel framed by up to eight or nine borders. The centre might be a pieced or appliquéd block or a square of printed cloth. Specially printed panels were a feature of early nineteenth-century medallion quilts and often commemorated an event of national importance, such as the Battle of Trafalgar, or bore the portrait of a royal personage. Sometimes the central panels would be embroidered.

The borders were usually composed of basic geometric shapes – rectangles, squares, triangles – as can be seen in the quilt opposite. This was made in the north of England in the Newcastle area at the beginning of this century. The fabrics are cotton prints and the quilting is in an all-over pattern. An unusual feature is the outlining of a number of pieces with the narrow strips of Turkey Red cotton.

The recently made top on page 75 is very much in the Victorian tradition of recycling clothing. The fabrics are lightweight wools and wool/cotton mixtures – sections cut from children's dresses and men's suits.

Opposite: Medallion quilts were very popular in the nineteenth century, although this one was completed at the beginning of King Edward VII's reign. It was worked by Mrs Elizabeth Robinson of Newcastle-upon-Tyne. The fabrics are pink, blue and yellow cotton prints with Turkey Red used to outline some shapes

Below: Medallion quilts were very popular in the 1880s. This one cleverly uses triangles and strips of patchwork to give a geometric framed effect

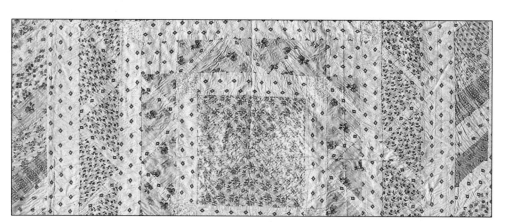

MEDALLION QUILT

It takes a considerable time to collect together enough fabrics of the right colourings and designs to make a piece like this, but it is well worth the effort and careful selection involved. Instead of woollen fabrics you might choose cotton. Medallion designs, such as this, are made up by working from the centre outwards, starting with the central square, adding borders to two opposite sides, then adding borders to the other two sides to complete a larger square. This is repeated until the whole piece is finished. Work this design using the American method (see page 96).

Size

85in (2.12m) square

MATERIALS

Scraps of lightweight wool, wool/cotton mixtures or cotton fabric in your chosen colourings – half of them printed and half in suiting. (The minimum usable size of fabric for this patchwork is 6in (15cm) square.) Matching thread.

ORDER OF WORK

No templates are given for this design as it is made up entirely of squares, triangles and rectangles.

The design seen here is based on a 5in (12.5cm) grid, (i.e., 5in (12.5cm) squares), 5×10in (12.5×25cm) and 15×5in (37.5×12.5cm) rectangles, and two sizes of right-angled triangles (half squares) with short sides measuring 5in (12.5cm) and 7½in (18.8cm).

Make templates for each of these shapes (see page 95 for making templates). Cut out the following, adding ¼in (6mm) seam allowance, with the squares and rectangles on the straight grain and the triangles with two short sides on the straight grain: 8 larger triangles (for centre panel) in printed fabric; 60 smaller triangles in printed wool and 28 in suiting; 40 squares in printed wool and 96 in suiting; 4 larger rectangles in suiting; 44 smaller rectangles in printed fabric.

Make up the patchwork, following the pattern. Start by making up the central medallion, sewing the triangles together in pairs and then making up into a square. Add a rectangle on two opposite sides. Then join a square to each end of another two rectangles and add one of the resulting strips to each of the two remaining sides of the square. Continue adding borders to the ever-increasing square in a similar way until the patchwork is complete, pressing as you go.

Opposite: This modern quilt is very much in the Victorian mode, both in colouring and design. In the tradition of patchwork, it is made from pieces of fine wool suitings and printed dress fabrics.

Diagram showing the arrangement of the shapes and fabrics for a modern Medallion quilt

SMALL GIFTS

In the hands of Victorian ladies of leisure, patchwork evolved from a utilitarian skill into a decorative craft. They made all kinds of small items from chair backs and cushions to tea cosies and bags. Clothing has often been ornamented with patchwork and it was even used to decorate a pair of gloves. One of the favourite small items made in patchwork was a pin cushion.

This chapter is devoted to designs for a number of small gifts – pin cushions, sachets, decorative Christmas balls and greetings cards. Making small articles like these is a good way of experimenting with designs and colours.

Opposite: Small gifts made from patchwork are a pleasure to make and a joy to receive. These colourful Christmas baubles and scented Suffolk Puff sachets would make delightful presents

Right: Both decorative and useful, these pin-cushions might have featured in a Victorian parlour

STRIP PIN CUSHIONS

These pin cushions demonstrate the versatility of strip patchwork. They are all made from the same patchwork 'fabric', assembled in three different ways. The strips may be joined together by hand or by machine.

Size

Each cushion measures approximately 4in (10cm) square.

MATERIALS

Scraps of cotton fabric in a range of colourings and patterns at least 12in (30cm) wide.
Matching thread
Stuffing

ORDER OF WORK

Cut the fabric into strips ¾in (2cm) to 1¼in (3cm) wide. Cut all strips on the straight grain.

Seam allowance ¼in (6mm).
Sew sufficient strips together along the long sides to make up a fabric measuring approximately 6×12in (15×30 cm) for each pin cushion. (A piece of fabric of 12×18in (30×45cm) will be enough for the back and front of three cushions.) Press.

For the vertical-stripe cushion cut two 4½in (11.5cm) squares on the straight – one for the back and one for the front. Make up into a cushion.

For the diagonal-strip cushion cut two 4½in (11.5cm) squares on the cross of the fabric. Make up into a cushion.

For the four-square cushion cut four 2½in (6.5cm) squares on the cross. Sew them together. Make up a second side in the same way. Sew the two together to make a cushion.

Pincushions were a popular Victorian gift and were often made not only for women friends and members of the family but sometimes for men also. These pincushions can be made with quite small scraps of fabric and although these have been made from cotton, luxurious fabrics, such as silk or brocade, could be used for a special gift

MINI-BLOCK PIN CUSHIONS

These two cushions are small versions of block patterns – other designs can be worked out on graph paper. The pin cushions can be made by either the English or American method, but it is easier to work small shapes like this by hand rather than by machine.

Size
Each cushion is 3in (7.5cm) square.

MATERIALS

Small scraps of cotton fabric in a range of colours and patterns.
Matching thread
Polyester filling

ORDER OF WORK

The patterns for the cushions are full-size and can also be used to make templates for the various shapes. Allow ¼in (6mm) seam allowance when cutting out fabric. (See page 95 for making templates.)
Cut out the shapes for each cushion, with square patches cut on the straight

grain and triangles having two short sides on the straight grain. Assemble the blocks and make up into pin cushions. It is not necessary to have the back and front of each cushion the same.

Trace the patterns below to make templates for the mini-block pincushions illustrated above

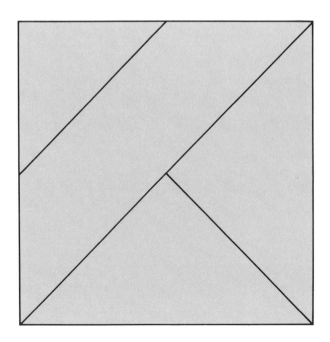

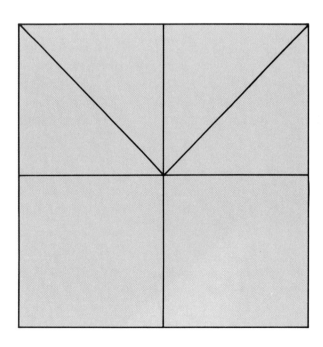

SUFFOLK PUFF SACHETS

Suffolk Puffs are sometimes used to make items such as crib quilts and tea cosies. Here, tiny puffs are made into little bags for pot-pourri. This type of patchwork does not require papers and is always worked by hand.

Size
Approximately 4in (10cm) diameter.

MATERIALS

⅛yd (11.5cm) of 36in (90cm)-wide printed cotton lawn
Matching thread
Scrap of muslin, approximately 5×10in (12.5×25cm)
Pot-pourri
½yd (45cm) of narrow ribbon

ORDER OF WORK

Make a circular template 3in (7.5cm) in diameter. Cut 2 muslin circles and make up into a round cushion shape, taking ¼in (6mm) seams. Loosely fill with pot pourri.

Using the same template, cut out 14 circles in printed cotton lawn.

Turn a ⅛in (3mm) hem round the edges and sew with running stitches (Fig 1). Draw up the stitches. Fasten off the thread end.

Work the other 13 circles in the same way. Oversew seven of the puffs together where they touch, gathered side upwards, to make a rosette shape (Fig 2).

Make up another rosette in the same way, using the remaining seven puffs. With wrong sides facing, sew the two rosettes together with a few oversewing stitches, slipping the muslin bag inside as you work. Add a ribbon loop for hanging.

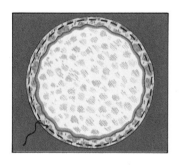

Turn a ⅛in (3mm) hem on the circles and gather up with small running stitches

Oversew 7 puffs together at the points where they touch to make a rosette shape

Delicate sachets, filled with
pot-pourri, made up from
rosettes of Suffolk Puffs, are
almost too pretty to be hidden
away in drawers.

CHRISTMAS BAUBLES

Balls made in Somerset patchwork make perfect Christmas decorations when seasonal red and green printed fabrics are used. However, colours to match any individual decorative scheme can be used instead.

Size
Approximately 3in (7.5cm) diameter

MATERIALS

¼yd (23cm) each of two contrasting cotton fabrics
½in (12mm) pins, called Lills
3in (7.5cm) soft ball (expanded poly-styrene) suitable for taking pins (available from crafts outlets)
Pencil
Tape measure
Narrow ribbon (optional)

ORDER OF WORK

Using the pencil and tape measure, mark the two poles of the ball and the circumference. Divide the ball into eight equal sections from pole to pole. Cut out 24 2½in (6cm) squares from one of the fabrics and 32 from the other fabric on the straight grain.
Take a square of fabric and fold it in half right sides together. Press. Fold down the creased corners to meet each other and damp-press to make a right-angled triangular patch. (Make sure the folds are accurate. Fig 1.) Repeat with the remaining squares.
Take four folded patches of the same colour and push a pin through their four points. Press the pin into the top of the ball.
Spread out the patches to align with the marked sections on the ball. Secure the bases of the patches with pins (Fig 2).
Take eight patches of the contrasting colour. Push a pin through the point of each patch. Pin the patches into place on top of the first row but lower down the ball, working in opposite pairs and covering previous raw edges and pins (Figs 3 and 4).
Add two more rows of eight patches, alternating the colours on each row.
Repeat the process on the other half of the ball.
Cut a length of fabric long enough to go round the circumference of the ball and wide enough to cover the raw edges and pins, plus a ¼in (6mm) allowance for turnings.
Turn in the allowance along the two long edges and press.
Position the strip around the ball, turn in the raw ends and pin in place.
If you wish to hang up the ball, tie a ribbon around and secure it with a pin.

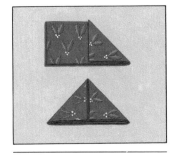

Fold the square, then fold down the corners to meet

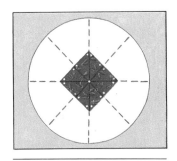

Pin 4 patches together and push into the top of the ball

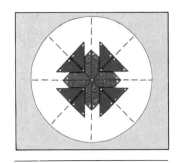

Add 8 more patches and pin at point and base

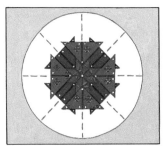

Continue, adding patches, covering previous patches and pins

Christmas baubles made in Somerset patchwork using fabrics in seasonal colours

SOMERSET PATCHWORK CARDS

Greeting cards can be made in much the same way, stitching the patches on to a piece of fabric, instead of a ball, and sticking that to a piece of card using all-purpose glue.

MATERIALS

Greetings card with a cut-out window
Square of white cotton fabric (a little larger than the window in the card)
⅛yd (11cm) each of two contrasting cotton fabrics
Matching thread
Pencil and ruler

ORDER OF WORK

Fold the square of white fabric in half, press. Open out and refold in half the other way, press. Repeat, making two diagonal folds. Open out the fabric and press lightly so that the fold lines can still be seen. (Alternatively, mark the divisions with pencil and ruler or with lines of basting stitches.)

Cut 2½in (6cm) squares, folding and pressing them as for the ball on page 83.

Position the first four patches in the centre, securing them with small stitches (instead of pins).

Continue adding patches, as for the ball, until the area of patchwork is slightly larger than the window in the card.

Glue the patchwork inside the card so that it lies behind the window when the card is folded.

NOTE Ribbon can be used for Somerset patchwork if you prefer and has an attractive, shimmering look to it. Use 1¼in (31mm)-wide ribbon and omit the first fold.

Opposite: Somerset patchwork, also known as Folded Star patchwork, can be used to good effect when mounted to make greetings cards. Cotton fabrics have been used here, but if you prefer, use a fabric with a silky finish. Ribbon can also be used

Right: Detail of the star motif on the greetings cards

CHRISTMAS
SAMPLER

A patchwork sampler is a good way of trying out different designs and colour schemes while creating a decorative hanging which will give pleasure for years to come.

This modern Christmas sampler was a group effort, with different people making the blocks and one sewing it into a hanging. There are six blocks in all, but only four different patterns; three are Diamond Stars in a variety of colour combinations. The completed sampler was outline-quilted close to the edges of the stars, along the seams around the edge of each block and between the borders.

Right: The Victorian home at Chrismas time became a hive of activity with all the family helping prepare the various seasonal trimmings, from Christmas puddings to patchwork gifts

Opposite: A Christmas sampler like this could make a family project, with each member making up blocks. Once completed, the sampler makes a memorable Christmas decoration which will be used and treasured for years. The designs for the blocks could also be used to make festive cushions

CHRISTMAS STAR SAMPLER

A variety of Christmas-motif cotton prints was used on the blocks – three or four on each. When the sampler was assembled, the blocks were separated by 1in (2.5cm)-wide strips of fabric. Then the piece was framed with more strips – 1in (2.5cm), ½in (1.2cm), 1¾in (4.5cm) and ½in (12mm)-wide – to make the four borders.

The Diamond Star block is illustrated below and the other three are on pages 90–91.

Trace off shapes for working all four blocks are given on the opposite page. Make up the blocks, by hand or machine, using the American method.

Size

The blocks are 7⅞in (20cm) square
The finished sampler measures approximately 24½×33in (62×84cm)

Trace the shapes on the opposite page to construct the four blocks for the Christmas Sampler

Below: Diamond Star Block

MATERIALS

8in (20cm) squares of Christmas-motif fabrics
⅛yd (11cm) of 36in (90cm)-wide fabrics in three different colours (for the borders)
Matching sewing threads

ORDER OF WORK

The templates are the finished size; add ¼in (6mm) seam allowance when cutting out fabric.

Diamond Star blocks This design is based on a 4×4 grid with the squares divided into equilateral triangles to make the star. In two of the blocks in the sampler, the four corners are also composed of equilateral triangles. In the third, the corners are squares. Cut triangles with two sides on the straight grain. Cut squares with all sides on the straight grain.

Using template (A), cut out 8 triangles from the first printed fabric, 8 from the second, 12 from the third and 4 from the fourth. (Alternatively, cut out 8 in each colour and 4 squares (template (B)) in the third colour.)

Following the block pattern assemble the triangles in pairs to make squares. Press. Assemble the block following the pattern. Press.

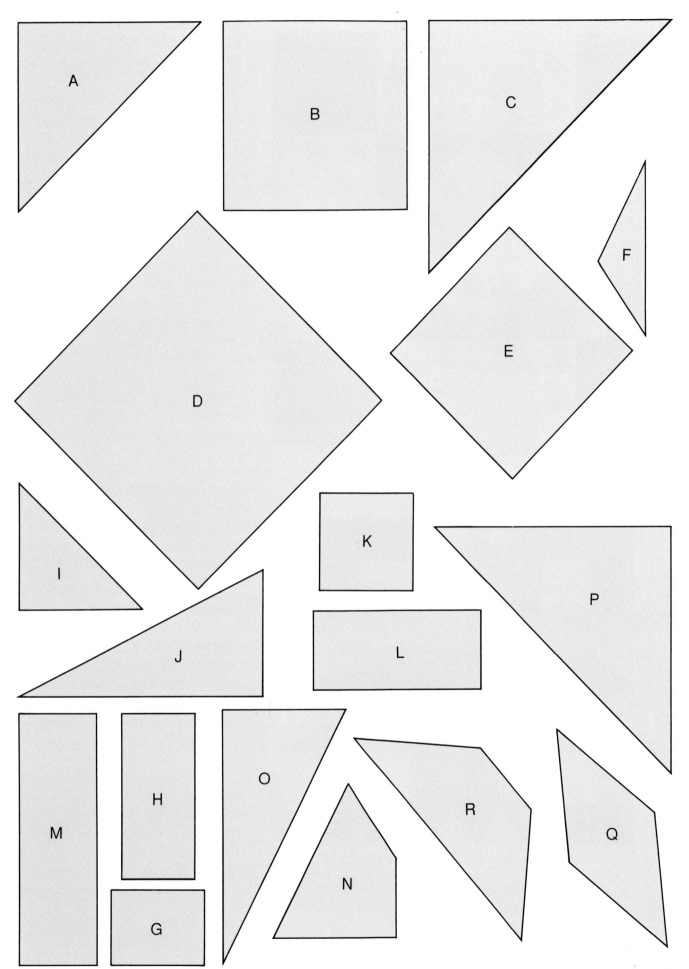

Top: Ribbon Star block
Above: Star-on-Diamond block

Ribbon Star block Cut triangles with two sides on the straight grain and squares with all sides on the straight grain.

Using template (A), cut out 8 triangles in the first printed fabric and 4 in the second.

Using template (B), cut out 4 squares in the second printed fabric.

Using template (C), cut out 4 larger triangles in the third printed fabric.

Using template (D), cut out 1 central square in the first fabric.

Following the pattern, assemble the block. Start with the central square and sew a triangle (A) in the second fabric to each of the two opposite sides. Repeat with the other two sides. Press. This makes a larger square.

Sew a triangle (A) in the first fabric to each side of one of the larger triangles (C). Press. Repeat with the remaining triangles to make four rectangles.

Sew a rectangle to each of two opposite sides of the square. Press.

Sew a square (B) to each end of one of the remaining rectangles. Press. Repeat with the remaining patches.

Sew one of the strips just made along the top of the block and one along the bottom to complete the design. Press.

Star-on-Diamond block

This is a quite complex nine-patch design, with each 2½in (6.3cm) patch made up of five or six separate pieces. Cut out fabric with at least two sides on the straight grain, except for the (F) pieces, where the longest side is on the straight grain.

From the first colour, cut out the following: using template (E), 1 piece; using template (F), 8 pieces (reversing the template for 4 of them); using template (G), 4 pieces; using template (H), 4 pieces.

From the second colour, cut out the following: using template (I), 4 pieces; using template (J), 8 pieces.

From the third colour, cut out the following: using template (K), (L),

(M), 4 pieces each; using template (N), 8 pieces (reversing template for 4 of them).

Following the pattern, make up each of the nine patches in turn. Press. Sew the patches together in three strips of three. Press. Sew the three strips together to complete the block. Press.

Starburst block

This is a four-patch design. The patches are identical. From the first and second fabrics, cut out the following: using template (P), 4 pieces of each; using template (Q), 4 pieces of each; using template (R), 4 pieces of each. From the third and fourth fabrics, cut out the following: using template (Q), 4 pieces of each.

Following the pattern, make up the first patch. Sew two of the (Q) pieces to one of the (R) pieces to make a diagonal strip. Press. Repeat with two more (Q) pieces and another (R) piece. Press. Sew one strip to one (P) piece and the second to another (P) piece. Press. This make two triangles. Sew the two triangles together to form a square patch. Press.

Repeat the whole process with the other four patches.

Making up the sampler

A ¼in (6mm) seam allowance is included on the border and trellis strips. Cut all strips on the straight grain.

Using one of the border fabrics, cut out 8 8⅜×1½in (21.2cm×37mm) strips. Arrange the blocks into two strips of three with lattice strips between them and at top and bottom. Stitch, then press. From the same border fabric, cut three 28⅛×1½in (71.2cm×37mm) strips. Sew the two strips of blocks together with one long lattice strip between them and another on each remaining long side. Press.

Using another border fabric, cut two 19¼×1in (48.7×2.5cm) strips.

Starburst block

Sew one strip to each short side of the sampler. Press.

Using the same fabric, cut two 29⅛×1in (73.8×2.5cm) strips.

Sew one strip to each long side of the sampler. Press.

Using a third border fabric, cut two strips 20¼×2¼in (51.2×5.6cm) and two strips 32⅝×2¼in (82.6×5.6cm).

Sew one of the shorter strips to each short side of the sampler. Press.

Sew one of the longer strips to each remaining side of the sampler. Press.

Using the second border fabric once more, cut two 23¾×1½in (60.1cm ×37mm) strips and two 34⅝×1½in (87.6×37mm) strips. Sew one of the shorter strips to each short side of the sampler. Press. Sew one of the longer ones to each of the remaining sides.

NOTE The outer border is cut with a wider seam allowance on the outer edge so that the front fabric can be taken to the back to bind the edges if desired (see page 99).

TECHNIQUES

There are not many rules in patchwork. Different people work in different ways and 'right' and 'wrong' do not really apply. In general, use the way of working that suits you best.

The essential rule, however, is accuracy and this applies to all stages, from cutting templates to marking and stitching the fabric. Otherwise you can find yourself with all sorts of problems.

One of the joys of the craft is its adaptability. As you become more accustomed to doing patchwork and progress from the smaller articles to the larger tablecloth and quilts in this book, you will probably want to make your own templates and create your own designs. By following the techniques in this chapter, you will be assured of success in this absorbing and satisfying hobby.

FABRICS

Firmly-woven fabrics are the best for patchwork – dress-weight cottons, wool and cotton mixtures, fine wools, silks and velvets. The last two are more difficult to work with, but can be used to stunning effect.

In any one piece of work, use fabrics of similar weight so that they will wear evenly – usually all cottons or all wools. With some techniques, such as Log Cabin, similar weights are not so critical because the pieces are mounted on to a foundation fabric which compensates for slight differences. Dissimilar fabrics can also be used for Crazy patchwork because this is usually used for smaller, decorative items and part of its charm is the variety of fabrics chosen.

In addition, if an item is quilted this will stabilize the patchwork and will also make it more hardwearing.

It is acceptable – and very traditional – to recycle fabrics for patchwork. On the whole, however, it is best not to mix old and new fabrics in one piece of work. The old pieces will wear out more quickly than the new and the new, stronger, fabrics will tend to pull away from the old ones, causing the seams to fray.

Straight grain: Cut out patches with at least one edge on the straight grain of the fabric. When cutting fabrics for blocks, ensure that sides adjacent to right angles are on the straight grain, e.g. cut right-angled triangles with two short sides on the straight grain. This is necessary to ensure a good shape when making up the block. It is particularly important to have all four outer edges of the block on the straight grain.

Sometimes, as in the case of the cushion made from squares and triangles on page 22 you may decide to break the rule to make a particular use of a fabric. However, this is not advisable when making up a large piece of work.

EQUIPMENT

Patchwork does not require much in the way of tools and equipment and you probably already have most of them in your sewing box. There are, however, various aids to marking and cutting out which you may want to invest in if you intend to do a lot of patchwork.

All types of patchwork can be sewn by hand but where straight seams or gradual curves are involved, it is possible, and often preferable, to use a sewing machine.

NEEDLES: For hand sewing, everyone has their own favourites but, in general, choose a needle as fine and as short as you can comfortably work with.

In Victorian times, drapers' shops sold clothing, boots and shoes as well as bedlinens, fabrics and haberdashery. In shops like this, women could buy all they needed for quiltmaking, from needles and thread to fabrics and wadding

A piece of patchwork like this relies for its success on choosing just the right area of a fabric design. A window template makes this task easy

THREAD: Pure cotton thread is best as synthetic fibres tend to stretch in sewing.

When working by hand choose the thread colour to suit the patches being joined. If you are sewing a light patch to a darker, match the thread to the darker colour as dark on light is less obtrusive then light on dark.

When machine sewing, it is a nuisance to be continually changing thread, so pick a colour which predominates in the work.

PINS: Use fine pins – those sold as 'Wedding and Lace Pins' are ideal – to avoid marking the fabric. For the same reason, do not leave pins in the work longer than is absolutely necessary.

PENCILS AND RULERS: Use an ordinary lead pencil for drawing out templates and marking fabric. On some fabrics a coloured pencil may be better for contrast and in such cases choose either blue or yellow. You will also need a metal ruler when drawing out templates.

SCISSORS: Have three pairs of scissors for patchwork: good dressmaking scissors for cutting fabric, a small pair of embroidery scissors for trimming thread ends etc. and a separate pair of scissors for cutting patchwork papers from thin card.

CUTTING BOARD AND CRAFT KNIFE: These are useful for cutting papers and essential if you are making your own templates.

SANDPAPER: Fine sandpaper is invaluable for smoothing the edges of home-made templates.

TEMPLATES

There are two types of templates used for patchwork. Solid templates are used for marking out fabric and for cutting papers (Fig 1). Window templates are used for positioning patches on a specific area and for cutting fabric (Fig 2).

Although it is not essential to use a window template this is a very useful aid for cutting the fabric accurately and for selecting the exact part of a fabric design you wish to use. A window template is the same shape as the solid one, but is ¼in (6mm) larger all round, to include the seam allowance. It is also see-through in the centre (i.e., only the ¼in (6mm) border is solid).

MAKING YOUR OWN TEMPLATE: It is quite simple to make your own templates using the trace-off shapes in this book. They can be made from thick card or, if you intend to use the shape often, from see-through plastic. The latter is sold in sheets, either plain or marked with a grid.

If you are using card, accurately trace off the template you require, using a sharp pencil and a ruler. Paste the tracing on to card and cut out, using a craft knife, ruler and cutting board. Smooth the edges with sandpaper. If you are using plastic, lay this over the appropriate template pattern and trace off and then cut out.

It is a good idea to make a window template for each shape in your patchwork. Draw round the solid template on a piece of card. Draw another line all around ¼in (6mm) from the first. Using a craft knife and ruler and a cutting board, cut away the centre shape, then cut around the outer line. Smooth the edges with sandpaper.

BOUGHT TEMPLATES: Ready-made templates can be obtained in a wide range of sizes and shapes. They are usually sold in sets of a solid metal template and a plastic window template.

The solid template is used for cutting papers and for marking out fabric

The window template enables the exact area of fabric to be chosen and includes a ¼in (6mm) seam allowance for cutting fabric

PAPERS

These are used for working the English method of sewing patchwork. Although they are known as 'papers' they should not be cut from notepaper or the pages of a magazine. These are far too thin and pliable and can cause inaccuracies in the work. Greetings cards, however, are ideal. They are the right weight to ensure accuracy and make sewing easy.

Papers may be cut with scissors or with a craft knife and cutting board, whichever you find easiest.

It is sometimes said that one should never pencil round the template before cutting out papers, but should hold the template firmly against the card and cut out with the blade of the scissors hard up against the template. It is, however, acceptable to draw round if the pencil point is very sharp. Angle the pencil into the template so the line is absolutely accurate.

Never cut some papers one way and some another in the same piece of work. You will get differences in sizes which will lead to trouble at the joining stage.

SEWING TECHNIQUES

Basically, there are two different methods of making up patchwork, with and without papers. The first technique, known as the English method, is always sewn by hand. The second, known as the American method, can be worked by hand or by sewing machine.

English method

This is used for almost any shape of patch. Use a window template to mark the cutting line on the wrong side of the fabric. (There is no need to mark out the sewing line as you are using the papers to make the shape.) Cut out the shape. Place a paper centrally on the wrong side of the fabric shape and pin the two together (Fig 1). Fold over the seam allowance and baste in place, paying particular attention to the corners (Fig 2). Wide-angled shapes are the easiest to work with; sharp angled ones are a little more difficult (Fig 3).

To join two patches together, place them right sides together. Knot the thread end and begin just in from the corner. Oversew along the edge to be joined with tiny stitches taken on the very edge of the fold, sewing back towards the corner before working along the seam. End by stitching back along the seam for a short distance (Fig 4). The weakest point of this type of patchwork is where three shapes meet. To lessen the problems, never stitch along more than two adjacent sides without fastening off the thread end. It also helps to reinforce corners with a few extra stitches. For the same reason, it is advisable to leave the papers in place until the whole patchwork is completed.

American method

This is the ideal technique for block patterns which usually involve only straight seams.

HAND SEWING: Papers are not used with this technique. Mark both the cutting and sewing lines on the wrong side of the fabric making sure that the sewing lines are absolutely accurate.

Place two patches right sides together and pin (Fig 5). Knot the thread end and work two or three back stitches, then sew along the seam with small running stitches, making a back stitch every few stitches. Finish with back stitches (Fig 6). Sew from raw edge to raw edge.

NOTE If you are joining shapes which involve working round corners (i.e., the Eight-Point Star design on page 44), take the seam along the sewing line only.

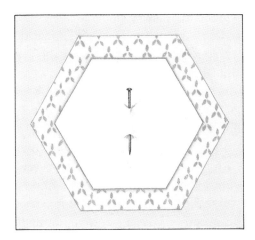

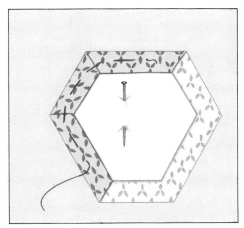

Pin the paper shape centrally to the fabric shape

Fold the seam allowance on to the paper and baste in place

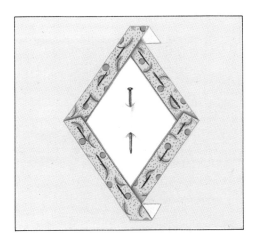

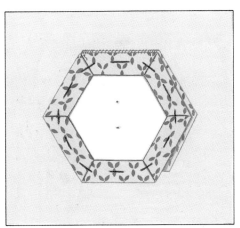

When working diamond patches, the corners need to be folded twice

Oversew patches together, right on the fold, taking tiny stitches through the fabric only

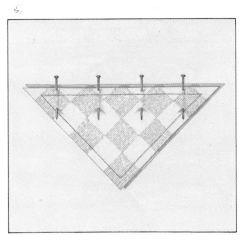

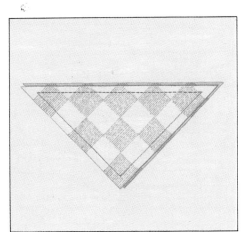

In the American method, patches are pinned together right sides facing

Patches are then joined with small running stitches, with a back stitch worked every few stitches

MACHINE SEWING: This is worked in the same way as for the hand method, but using a medium-length straight machine stitch.

There is an alternative way to work by machine, but the fabric must be very accurately cut. In this method there is no need to mark the sewing line. Simply use the width of the machine foot as a guide. (It must be exactly ¼in (6mm) wide, or you can mark the foot plate with masking tape ¼in (6mm) from the needle hole as a guide.)

Pressing

It is important to press seams as they are completed. Press seams open or to one side. If you intend to quilt the work along the seam the latter method is preferable.

COVERLETS AND QUILTS

There are two sorts of bedcovers — coverlets and quilts. A coverlet is usually just two layers, a top and a lining, the layers held together either by knotting or by quilting. A quilt consists of three layers, a top and a lining with an interlining in between, the layers held together either by knotting or quilting.

LINING FABRIC: The choice of fabric is up to you. If the work is to be quilted, choose one that is light in weight. It is also a good idea to select an attractive fabric to complement the patchwork as you will probably see almost as much of the lining as of the top.

INTERLININGS: There are many different interlinings available ranging from fine, silk waddings to woven cottons and wools. Synthetic waddings, sold in a range of different weights, are suitable for most purposes. Woven cotton domette interlining and flannelette sheeting are other good choices.

A tempting display of quilts and coverlets featured in Hans Christian Anderson's fairy tale *The Real Princess*

If you want to be very traditional, you might like to use an old blanket as interlining. This is much heavier of course but is very nice to work on if you are quilting.

BASTING THE LAYERS TOGETHER: Whether you are making a coverlet or a quilt, the preparation is the same, and vital for good results. Give yourself plenty of room to work. The floor is ideal if you have not got a table of suitable size. Lay the lining out flat, wrong side up, and place the interlining (if you are using one) over it. Finish with the top, right side up.

Work down the quilt, always in the same direction, smoothing out the layers and pinning them together every 2–4in (5–10cm). Baste the layers together with rows of basting the same distance apart. Remove the pins. Repeat across the work, so that you finish up with a grid of basting.

ATTACHING THE LINING: A traditional way of joining the layers together is by knotting. The knotted ends can be on either the right or wrong side.

Working with doubled thread, in a matching or contrasting colour, make knots every 4–9in (10–23cm). For each knot, take a small stitch through all layers, leaving a long end. Make another stitch on the same spot (Fig 1). Then tie off the ends in a reef knot. Cut off the ends about ½in (12mm) from the knot (Fig 2).

NOTE The knots may blend in with the patchwork or may contrast with it as a decoration. In the latter case you could use several threads together of different colours and leave the ends long.

FINISHING THE EDGES: There are numerous ways of doing this. The classic way to finish a coverlet or quilt is simply to turn in the seam allowance all around the work on both top and lining and sew the edges together with running stitch.

Knotting layers together: take a small stitch through all layers, then make another stitch at the same spot

Tie off the thread ends in a reef knot, cut ends ½in (12mm) from the knot

Finishing edges: hem the quilt edges, mitring the corners for a neat finish

If you wish you can insert a fabric frill or lace edging between the layers before stitching.

Alternatively, bring the lining fabric over to the front and hem into place to 'bind' the edge. Or take the front fabric to the back and stitch down in the same way. In either case you will need to make a mitred corner (Fig 3).

NOTE When working, use either imperial or metric measurements. Do not mix the two.

FINISHING TOUCHES

Although a piece of patchwork is a delightful thing in itself there are other techniques which can be used to embellish and complement the work, in particular, quilting and appliqué. Embroidery stitches can be an attractive addition and were particularly popular with Victorian ladies (who sometimes used them to excess). Four of the most popular are given on page 105.

Although this book is mainly concerned with patchwork, a basic knowledge of these three complementary crafts will give wider scope to your work.

QUILTING

The most secure, and the most decorative, way to hold two or three layers of fabric together when making a bedcover is by quilting. It is also a lovely technique for adding richness and depth to other patchwork articles – cushions, bags and items of clothing.

The patterns
The simplest way to create a quilting pattern on a piece of patchwork is just to outline all or part of the design. To do this either quilt along the seam lines, or on one or both sides.

For a richer, more elaborate, effect, you might like to work one or more of the traditional quilting patterns – fans, roses, hearts, leaves or feathers – working within the different patchwork shapes. Some trace-off patterns are given on pages 106–109. With a patchwork design which incorporates both plain and patterned fabrics you might decide to quilt just the plain ones. Alternatively, and particularly with bedcovers, you may prefer to work out a design, which is quite independent of the patchwork, to cover the whole surface.

This quilt is typical of the beautiful work done in the north of England in the nineteenth and early twentieth centuries. It was made by a widow, Mrs Stewart, who kept her family by quilting

EQUIPMENT

FRAMES: If the layers of fabric have been properly basted together (see page 00) a frame is unnecessary – you can work in the hand. You may, however, like to use an embroidery hoop or a quilting hoop to hold the area you are working on. A quilting hoop is larger than an embroidery hoop and the sides are deeper, so it is more suitable for thicker pieces of work. But even with a hoop, the basting stage cannot be omitted.

NEEDLES: Short, quilting Betweens are the best choice.

THREAD: Choose special pure cotton, or cotton-covered quilting thread, available in a wide range of colours. Alternatively, ordinary pure cotton sewing thread can be used.

Some needleworkers wax their thread by pulling it over a piece of candle or beeswax to make it slide smoothly through the fabric. This is not necessary with purpose-made quilting thread.

THIMBLE: If you can use one, a thimble is a great help in pushing the needle through the work without damaging your fingers.

MARKERS: In some regions, patterns were marked on the fabric with chalk, in others, blue pencil was the favourite marker. A pale blue pencil is still favoured by many modern-day quilters as it tends to merge into the background once the design has been quilted. On some fabrics, a yellow pencil is a good choice.

An ordinary lead pencil, however, works on almost all colours – even dark ones. Use a lightly-dotted line, rather than a solid one, and it will be undetectable once the quilting is finished. Another traditional and effective way to mark out a pattern, is by

'drawing' round the shape with the point of a blunt needle.

For outline quilting, you can buy ¼in (6mm)-wide guide-tape which is slightly sticky on one side. This is laid with one edge on the seam and stitches are worked close to the other edge, giving perfectly even quilting lines. The tape is then lifted from the fabric. (It can be reused if you are careful.)

TEMPLATES: You can cut your own templates quite easily from card or plastic (in a similar way to cutting patchwork shapes, see page 95). There is a selection of traditional designs on pages 106–109, or you might like to invent some of your own. When making the template, cut out along the outline and fill in the detail free-hand when marking out the fabric.

It is also possible to buy ready-made quilting templates in a variety of designs and sizes. These are usually made from plastic and their advantage is that because they have been cut out like stencils they include all the sewing lines.

Marking out the design

Quilters differ as to whether the design should be marked on the fabric before or after basting the three layers together. It is certainly easier to draw on to the fabric if you have only one layer. On the other hand, the design may rub off with all the handling when smoothing, pinning and basting the layers together. (And you might change your mind as to which areas you wish to quilt.)

In Victorian times patchwork was popular with all social classes, from the rich to the poor. This stunning quilt features in a Victorian painting, 'The Quilters'

Designs are marked out on the quilt top. Place the work on a firm, flat surface, position the template and draw lightly round it. Mark in the detail – leaf veins etc. – freehand.

Stitching

Work quilting either in the hand or in a hoop. If using a hoop, have the work slack to enable you to stitch easily.

The traditional quilting stitch is running stitch. The golden rule with quilting is to keep the stitches even; this is far more important than making them small.

Start by making a knot. Put the needle into the fabric from the top of the work, a little way away from the marked design. Take it into the layer of wadding. Then bring it up where you intend to start sewing and pull the thread until the knot goes through the top fabric and embeds itself in the wadding. Work running stitch along the marked line, through all three layers.

To fasten off, make a back stitch, then make a knot about 1in (2.5cm) from the last stitch. Make another back stitch, but take the needle through only the top and wadding. Bring it up a little way away from the line, pull the knot through into the wadding. Cut off the thread end so that it disappears into the work.

Every time you stop work, remove the hoop. If you leave the hoop in place for any length of time it may flatten the interlining and mark the fabric.

APPLIQUÉ

Frequently, patchwork patterns, such as the Flower Basket block on page 68, involve a small, amount of appliqué as well. On other occasions, a single patchwork motif may be made up and then appliquéd to another fabric (see the Rose cushion, page 61).

Detail of the quilt on page 105

There are a variety of different appliqué methods and three are given here – the standard, turned-in method, the Hawaiian method, which is excellent for attaching curved shapes, and the method for attaching a patchwork motif.

Standard method

Cut out the appliqué shape in fabric with ¼in (6mm) seam allowance. Cut out the finished shape in thin card without the seam allowance. Place the fabric shape face downwards, place the card template centrally on top. Turn the seam allowance on to the template and press, clipping curves and corners where necessary to ensure that they lie flat. Remove the template. Pin the appliqué motif right side up on the background fabric. Baste in position close to the edge. Stitch in place with small, neat hemming stitches. Remove the basting.

Hawaiian method

Trim the seam allowance on the appliqué shape to about ⅛in (3mm). Do not turn in the seam allowance; instead pin the shape in position on the background fabric, right side up.

Embroidery stitches illustrated here are chain stitch, feather stitch, herring-bone stitch and threaded herring-bone stitch

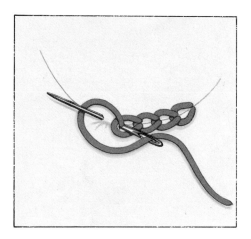

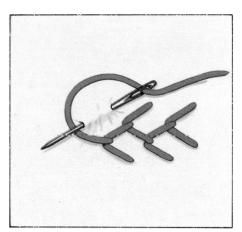

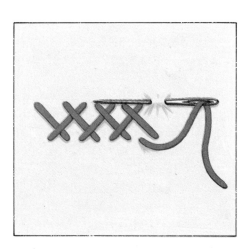

Opposite: Appliqué dominates this lovely quilt, made in Weardale in the north of England by Mrs Isabella Cruddas. The design shows a definite American influence although the colours are very much in the local tradition

Work a line of basting all around the shape, approximately ½in (12mm) in from the cut edge.

Work tiny hemming stitches all round the edge of the shape, pushing under the seam allowance as you go with the point of the needle. Remove the basting.

This sounds much more difficult than it is! It is quite straightforward once you get the hang of it.

Attaching a patchwork motif

DESIGNS MADE OVER PAPERS: Before removing the papers, press the work from the wrong side to firmly crease in the seam allowance. Snip the basting threads and remove the papers carefully. Position the motif right side up on the background fabric. Pin, baste and then hem in place as for the standard method.

EMBROIDERY STITCHES

CHAIN STITCH: The 'links' of the chain can be open and round or pulled tighter so that the 'link' chain closes. This stitch was used to decorate some of the seams on the Nine-Patch baby's quilt on page 51.

FEATHER STITCH: Can be worked in a straight line or around a curve. Take one stitch to the right of the line, the next to the left and so on. This is a useful stitch with which to decorate seams – particularly to work over the joins on Crazy patchwork.

HERRING-BONE STITCH: For the best effect, keep the spaces between the stitches even. This works well on Crazy patchwork and was one of the stitches used on the Grandmother's Fan quilt on page 40. It is a useful stitch as it can be used as the basis for a variety of composite stitches, such as Threaded Herring-bone stitch.

THREADED HERRING-BONE STITCH: Here a thread in a second colour is woven in and out of the herring-bone.

These traditional quilting designs can be used singly, or repeated across a quilt, or along a border. Trace the design from the page and transfer the lines to thin card to make a template. Mark round the shape on the fabric, using a pencil, or with the point of a blunt needle. Add the inner lines freehand.

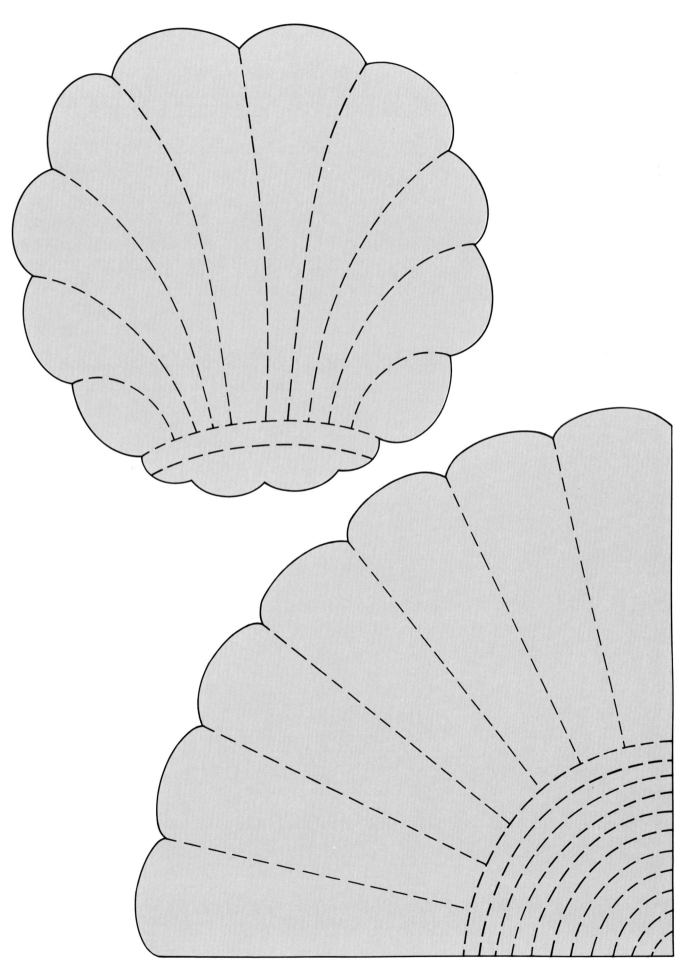

INDEX

ACKNOWLEDGEMENTS AND PICTURE CREDITS

I should like to thank the following for helping to make this book possible: **Dorothy Bright**, **Adel Corcoran and Peter Thorogood** for the loan of their original pieces of patchwork, and **Maureen Lusted of Pantiles Spa Antiques**, Royal Tunbridge Wells, Kent for the loan of the doll's bed and teddy bear; **Josie Studd** who designed the Nine-Patch crib quilt; **Pat Salt** who designed the evening waistcoat and the pin cushions; **Dinah Travis** for her design of a medallion quilt, Suffolk Puff sachets and Somerset balls and cards; and **Pat Wernham** who created the Christmas sampler from blocks made by her and her fellow Beckenham quilters.

My gratitude goes also to the **Beamish North of England Open Air Museum** for allowing us to photograph many of its beautiful quilts, and some of the projects for this book, in such a delightful location and in particular to **Sharon Brown** for her help in smoothing our path. Thanks, too, to friends who allowed us to photograph in their houses.

Thank you to **Dinah Travis** and **Pat Salt** for giving me the benefit of their wide experience of teaching patchwork and quilting and for reading the text.

And, once again, thank you **Di Lewis** for the superb photographs. Finally, thank you to my family, particularly my husband **Jack Parker**, for their support.

The publishers would like to thank the following for providing photographs: 2, 20, 34, 39, 86, Bridgeman Art Library; 10, The President and Council of the Royal College of Surgeons of England; 15, Mary Evans Picture Library; 9, 24, 28, 35, 37 (bottom), 44, 66, 72, 88, 102, Beamish Museum; 56, Winterthur Museum; 98, Victoria & Albert Museum/E.T. Archive.